THE COAST OF ILLYRIA

The Coast of Illyria

A PLAY IN THREE ACTS BY

DOROTHY PARKER & ROSS EVANS

INTRODUCTION BY ARTHUR F. KINNEY

UNIVERSITY OF IOWA PRESS ❖ IOWA CITY

University of Iowa Press,
Iowa City 52242
Copyright © 1990 by the
University of Iowa
All rights reserved
Printed in the United States
of America
First edition, 1990

Design by Richard Hendel

Printed on acid-free paper

Library of Congress Cataloging-in-
Publication Data

Parker, Dorothy, 1893–1967.
  The Coast of Illyria: a play in
three acts/by Dorothy Parker and
Ross Evans; introduction by Arthur
F. Kinney.—1st ed.
    p. cm.
  ISBN 0-87745-273-3,
  ISBN 0-87745-288-1 (pbk.)
    1. Lamb, Charles, 1775–1834, in
fiction, drama, poetry, etc.
  2. Lamb, Mary, 1764–1847, in fic-
tion, drama, poetry, etc. I. Evans,
Ross. II. Title.
PS3531.A5855C65 1990
812'.52—dc20   89-20251
                                   CIP

CONTENTS

ACKNOWLEDGMENTS

In preparing the Introduction, I am grateful for permission to use the files of the Texas/Dallas History and Archives Division, Dallas Public Library, and for permission to cite from the records of the Edinburgh Festival Society, Ltd., as well as for information and counsel from the following: Romola Robb Allrud, Thomas Ashton, George Baxt, Arnaud d'Usseau, Lee R. Edwards, Richard Haven, Mary Heath, Michael Holohan, Robert Keefe, Jed Mace, Marion Meade, Charles Proudfit, Ursula Schaeffer, Helen Sheey, and Michael Woolf. I also wish to thank Mary Curran, my editor, and Richard Hendel for another striking design. Lydia and Christopher Martin helped with the proofing.

Portions of *The Ladies of the Corridor* are reprinted with the permission of the Columbia University Libraries; the original manuscript forms part of the Leah Salisbury Papers in the Rare Book and Manuscript Library, Columbia University. The photographs are from the Collection of the Texas/Dallas History and Archives Division, Dallas Public Library. Finally, permission to reprint *The Coast of Illyria* was kindly granted by the NAACP.

A.F.K.

INTRODUCTION

By Arthur F. Kinney

T*he Coast of Illyria*, long buried, forgotten, and unpublished until now, represents some of Dorothy Parker's finest and most mature work. The deeply felt theme of abandonment, which still gives to her bittersweet poetry its most haunting qualities, is combined with the rich understanding of despair that characterizes her prizewinning story "Big Blonde," now a classic, and her other fine play, written with Arnaud d'Usseau, *The Ladies of the Corridor*. But the issues raised in these other works—still the most memorable works she has left us—are explored in this play about Charles and Mary Lamb and their circle with a depth, a sensibility, and a subtlety unmatched in anything else she ever did. And like these other works, this too can be harrowingly autobiographical: *The Coast of Illyria* not only displays Dorothy Parker as the artist she aspired to be but also brings us closest to the woman herself.

For one thing, Romola Robb, the young actress hired by Margo Jones for her regional theater in Dallas for the 1948–49 season primarily to play the role of Mary Lamb, recalls that, during the two weeks of production when Parker and her putative coauthor Ross Evans sat through rehearsals rewriting and revising the script, she had the distinct impression that Parker saw herself, at least potentially, as Mary Lamb. Perhaps she even said as much.[1] In addition, Marion Meade suggests in her recent biography of Parker that the play draws mainly on her "painful psychological relationship with Alan Campbell, her former husband, whom she would shortly remarry."[2] Surely *The Coast of Illyria* is a play even more about Mary than about Charles, although it uses Charles, as well as Coleridge, Hazlitt, De Quincey, and others, to probe the character, the environment, and the circumstances that could periodically drive an intelligent and responsible woman to fits of madness.

From the start there could be little doubt that the story of Mary Lamb was profoundly tragic, a story that would concern

Parker. In its broadest outlines it was not dissimilar from the story of Hazel Morse, the "big blonde," or from that of the alcoholic Susan Hayward played in *Smash-Up—The Story of a Woman*, a movie of the filmscript that Parker had completed with Frank Cavett the year before for Walter Wanger. Where Parker first heard the story of Mary Lamb—and there are many possibilities, as we shall see—is not known. She could have found a helpful summary in *Mary Lamb*, an early account by Anne Gilchrist published in the "Famous Women" series that by its very nature would have attracted Parker. Gilchrist opens her book with a decisive thesis: "The story of Mary Lamb's life is mainly the story of a brother and sister's love; of how it sustained them under the shock of a terrible calamity, and made beautiful and even happy a life which must else have sunk into desolation and despair."[3] Though Parker and Evans treat the same subject in their play, their tone differs strikingly. The epigraph which they typed on the title page—"There were a brother and sister . . . who were shipwrecked off the coast of Illyria"—is an allusion to Shakespeare's *Twelfth Night*, which Mary is recasting for the Lambs' *Tales from Shakespeare* during the course of the play. Margo Jones put the epigraph in the program, recognizing that it is also an allusion to Parker and Evans's own play. "For Charles and Mary Lamb, the coast of Illyria is the edge of sanity or normalcy, for they have to live on the fringe of the world," Jones writes, and then she summarizes *The Coast of Illyria*:

> To save Mary from a mental institution (Bedlam, to be exact) after she has killed their mother, Charles agrees to take care of her for the rest of his life. The play considers the tragedy of Mary, a brilliant woman and a very warm person, who knows that she has periods of derangement. And it speaks of Charles's sacrifice, clearly illustrated when he has to break off his romance with the actress Fanny Kelly in order to devote his time to his diseased sister.[4]

Thus the title—perhaps even the donnée of the play—is likelier to have been derived from *The Lambs: A Story of Pre-Victorian England*, a popular account by Katharine Anthony that was published by Alfred A. Knopf in 1945, two years before

Parker wrote her play. Anthony cites a letter from Charles Lamb to Coleridge in which Lamb remarks, tellingly,

My heart is quite sunk, and I don't know where to look for relief. Mary will get better again; but her constantly being liable to such relapses is dreadful; nor is it the least of our evils that her case and all our story is so well known around us. We are in a manner *marked*. Excuse my troubling you; but I have nobody by me to speak to me. I slept out last night, not being able to endure the change and stillness. But I did not sleep well, and I must come back to my own bed. I am going to try to get a friend to come and be with me tomorrow. I am completely shipwrecked. My head is quite bad. I almost wish that Mary were dead.[5]

The year is 1800, but in *The Coast of Illyria* this period coalesces with Anthony's account of 1809.

If a soothsayer had been consulted by the Lambs, he would surely have told them to beware of the year 1809. It was the critical year of their joint lives. After a period of peace and security everything went wrong again in that particular twelvemonth. Mary was suddenly attacked by one of her most severe illnesses. That same summer, while Mary still tarried in the hospital, Charles was arrested for drunkenness. It happened on Sunday in a little village near London, whither Charles and a fellow clerk from [East] India House had gone for an outing. An excess of holiday spirits brought them in conflict with the local church elders and Lamb was put in the stocks. "A thing of naught"—as he afterwards dismissed it—"a fault of youth and warmer blood." In reality Lamb was thirty-four; he could scarcely plead youth in extenuation of his conduct. He might with more justice have pleaded Destiny—the awful Destiny of the house of Lamb. This and the narrow-mindedness of Little Barnet landed the celebrated Charles Lamb, on a fine Sunday morning in 1809, in the public stocks. And Mary was doing penance in a strait-jacket at Hoxton at the same time. The brother and sister had broken down simultaneously when, if ever strength and self-confidence might have been expected of them, this was the time.[6]

But in *The Coast of Illyria*, such a combination of events makes the shipwreck of brother and sister inescapable because her incipient madness drives him to drink and his alcoholism brings on her madness.

Despite the stark tragedy at its roots, *The Coast of Illyria* is nevertheless multivalent: sorrow is often displaced by joy and tenderness, and relief is often supplied by recognizable Parker wit—the puns and one-liners characteristic of the mordant if vulnerable tones of her poetry. Indeed, the play opens happily. Charles is courting Fanny Kelly, a successful actress at Drury Lane; they plan to announce their marriage when Mary, whose last illness has institutionalized her, returns home. Fanny no sooner leaves than Coleridge arrives—the self-destructive Coleridge, complaining about his own hellish pains of mind and body. Coleridge's anxiety and despair, his near-madness of speech and need for the laudanum which he carries with him, embody the tragedies of Mary and Charles: he is both an emblem of the play's impossible situation and a forewarning of what the remaining acts will unfold. Although Charles and Coleridge are offset in the first act by the lovely dignity of Mary, who appears cured, and the sweetness of the Lambs' permanent houseguest, George Dyer—who gave away all his money, Charles tells us, because his head is uniformly wrong while his heart is uniformly right—there is an underlying concern that Mary's mental stability is only temporary. Still, Parker and Evans know how to *enact* scenes: Charles must destroy the Hogarth picture of Bedlam on one of Mary's treasured glasses before she returns and so he smashes it in the fireplace; Coleridge places his vial of laudanum on the mantel to show he intends to abstain forever—and our eyes keep straying back to it; the Lambs' writing desk, always before us on the stage, stands neatly arranged but unused.

The deep and bitter tragedy of love too promising to be lost and too sensitive to withstand living, captured in the characterization of Coleridge in act 1, expands almost unbearably in act 2. As Fanny's gaiety opened the first act, so the promise of a Thursday night at the Lambs' with good food, sparkling conversation, and games of whist opens the second. But Hazlitt comes to complain of his wife's desertion of him. Before that, Coleridge arrives, and in time is introduced to Thomas De Quincey, a blond boy of nineteen who is learned in books and shares Coleridge's love for opium. To add to his troubles, Charles has bought for Mary all but one of the prints in a set of *A Rake's Progress* by Hogarth, only to learn that the gallery also delivered the Bedlam scene that might bring on her a permanent madness. Mrs. Kelly is horror-struck by the guests and leaves when Coleridge reads aloud from Charles's "Confessions of a Drunkard," for she will not allow her daughter to marry a man who is widely known as an alcoholic and, furthermore, is the brother of a girl who murdered their mother with a kitchen knife.

If the first act signifies paradise lost and the second act pandemonium, the third act is hell itself. A week has passed and Charles has been drinking day and night, for he has had no word from Fanny since her mother abruptly took her away the preceding Thursday night. When Fanny arrives to tell him that her mother had kept his letters of entreaty from her and that she has only now learned of his continued love for her, and when his employer, Mr. Wilberforce, arrives from the East India Company to announce that Charles has not been fired, as he thought, but given a pension for life so that he may devote all of his time to writing, things seem about to right themselves. Mary, however, cannot live without Charles; Fanny cannot live with them both. Charles wishes to be a married man and a father—to have a fuller life than that of a brother—but he cannot resign the responsibility for his sister, cannot commit her to Bedlam, which Hogarth has put before him (and us) in all its horror. As the play ends, Fanny leaves Charles, and Mary, threatened by the thought of their marriage, sinks into another period of insanity. Charles stands alone, asking for something to hate and hating the burden of being everything to his sweet sister, who cannot let him go lest she lose her mind in the giving.

The Coast of Illyria thus moves inexorably toward the awful awareness which comes to Charles and Mary of the fate that each suffers and that they seem destined also to share. It develops dramatically the personal, firsthand account of their situation by T. N. Talfourd, published in 1848 and excerpted for handy reference for Parker and Evans in a compilation of material on

the Lambs put together by Edmund Blunden for Leonard and
Virginia Woolf at the Hogarth Press about a decade before the
play. The salient passage reads,

His sister still remained in confinement in the asylum to
which she had been consigned on her mother's death—
perfectly sensible and calm,—and he was passionately desir-
ous of obtaining her liberty. The surviving members of the
family, especially his brother John, who enjoyed a fair income in the South Sea House, opposed her discharge;—and
painful doubts were suggested by the authorities of the parish, where the terrible occurrence happened, whether they
were not bound to institute proceedings, which must have
placed her life at the disposition of the Crown, especially as
no medical assurance could be given against the probable
recurrence of dangerous frenzy. But Charles came to her de-
liverance; he satisfied all the parties who had power to op-
pose her release, by his solemn engagement that he would
take her under his care for life; and he kept his word.
Whether any communication with the Home Secretary occurred before her release, I have been unable to ascertain; it
was the impression of Mr. Lloyd, from whom my own knowledge of the circumstances, which the letters do not ascertain, was derived, that a communication took place, on
which a similar pledge was given; at all events, the result
was, that she left the asylum and took up her abode for life
with her brother Charles. For her sake, at the same time, he
abandoned all thoughts of love and marriage.[7]

The tone of the play is darkened considerably as it rotates
around the emerging memory of the moment when Mary Lamb
suddenly plunged a kitchen knife through her mother's heart,
killing her instantly in full sight of her father and aunt. In this,
the play seems to take its final direction from De Quincey's essay "On Murder, Considered As One of the Fine Arts"—a work
named in *The Coast of Illyria* as a specific point of reference—in
which he proposes that "the final purpose of murder" when it is
"considered as a fine art, is precisely the same as that of tragedy,
in Aristotle's account of it; viz., 'to cleanse the heart by means
of pity and terror.' Now, terror there may be, but how can there

be any pity for one tiger destroyed by another tiger?"[8] In the instance of Mary Lamb, Parker and Evans seem to say, how does pity (which we are required to give sister and brother) manage such terror without diminishing the deed, the anguish of Mary and Charles, or their very real claims to some authentic portion of human dignity? And since those who surround the Lambs in *The Coast of Illyria* are, most of them, also practicing poets whose minds often range along the margins of discourse as well as the margins of consciousness where reality gives way to the imagination and to visions beyond, what does it say about their attraction to the Lambs, about their own genius, about the artist generally and the province and possibilities for art?

"Cast read ILLYRIA today," Margo Jones wired from Dallas to Dorothy Parker and Ross Evans in Hollywood on February 23, 1949; "It was exciting beyond words."[9] Romola Robb, the actress who played Mary Lamb, agrees; "it was terrifically exciting and powerful theater," she recalls.[10] The excitement and power both stem largely from the growing capacity of the characters in the play and of the members of the audience seeing it to comprehend the crime with which it means to come to terms.

The documents on which *The Coast of Illyria* and all other renderings of the Lambs' tragedy rest were conveniently collected by E. V. Lucas in his three-volume set of the letters of Charles Lamb and Mary Lamb published in 1935, a resource Parker and Evans might well have used. The first acknowledgment of the event, which occurred on September 22, 1796, comes in a letter written five days later on the afternoon or evening of September 27, when Charles informs Coleridge.

My dearest friend—White or some of my friends or the public papers by this time may have informed you of the terrible calamities that have fallen on our family. I will only give you the outlines. My poor dear dearest sister in a fit of insanity has been the death of her own mother. I was at hand only time enough to snatch the knife out of her grasp. She is at present in a mad house, from whence I fear she must be moved to an hospital. God has preserved to me my

senses,—I eat and drink and sleep, and have my judgment I
believe very sound. My poor father was slightly wounded,
and I am left to take care of him and my aunt. Mr. Norris of
the Bluecoat school has been very kind to us, and we have
no other friend, but thank God I am very calm and composed, and able to do the best that remains to do. Write,—as
religious a letter as possible—but no mention of what is
gone and done with—with me the former things are passed
away, and I have something more to do [than] to feel—
     God almighty

                              have us all in
                              his keeping.—

Lamb adds in a postscript that he has eradicated his past, burnt
all his poetry, and wishes Coleridge to publish none of it with
his, Charles's, "name or initial, and never send me a book, I
charge you."

The newspaper account to which Lamb refers in his letter
was that published in the *London Morning Chronicle* for September 26.

     On Friday afternoon the Coroner and a respectable Jury
sat on the body of a Lady in the neighbourhood of Holborn,
who died in consequence of a wound from her daughter the
preceding day. It appeared by the evidence adduced, that
while the family were preparing for dinner, the young lady
seized a case knife laying on the table, and in a menacing
manner pursued a little girl, her apprentice, round the room;
on the eager calls of her helpless infirm mother to forbear,
she renounced her first object, and with loud shrieks approached her parent.

     The child by her cries quickly brought up the landlord of
the house, but too late—the dreadful scene presented to him
the mother lifeless, pierced to the heart, on a chair, her
daughter yet wildly standing over her with the fatal knife,
and the venerable old man, her father, weeping by her side,
himself bleeding at the forehead from the effects of a severe
blow he received from one of the forks she had been madly
hurling about the room.

For a few days prior to this the family had observed some symptoms of insanity in her, which had so much increased on the Wednesday evening, that her brother early the next morning went in quest of Dr. Pitcairn—had that gentleman been met with, the fatal catastrophe had, in all probability, been prevented.

It seems the young Lady had been once before, in her earlier years, deranged, from the harassing fatigues of too much business.—As her carriage towards her mother was ever affectionate in the extreme, it is believed that to the increased attentiveness, which her parents' infirmities called for by day and night, is to be attributed the present insanity of this ill-fated young woman.

It has been stated in some of the Morning Papers, that she has an insane brother also in confinement—this is without foundation [although Charles had, many years previously, been placed in the ward at Hoxton for six weeks].

The Jury of course brought in their Verdict, *Lunacy*.

Lucas reports that the *Whitehall Evening Post* printed essentially the same story but with a new conclusion that ended all the discretion of the earlier account: "The above unfortunate person is a Miss Lamb, a mantua-maker, in Little Queen-street, Lincoln's-inn-fields. She has been, since, removed to Islington mad-house."[11]

Despite Charles's assertion that he felt "calm and composed," the state of his mind may have been, and for some time remained, unsettled. His next letter to Coleridge, on October 3, if less anxious, seems yet more strange.

My dearest friend, your letter was an inestimable treasure to me. It will be a comfort to you, I know, to know that our prospects are somewhat brighter. My poor dear dearest sister, the unhappy and unconscious instrument of the Almighty's judgments to our house, is restored to her senses; to a dreadful sense and recollection of what has past, awful to her mind, and impressive (as it must be to the end of life) but temper'd with religious resignation, and the reasonings of a sound judgment, which in this early stage knows how to distinguish between a deed committed in a transient fit of

frenzy, and the terrible guilt of a Mother's murther. I have
seen her. I found her this morning calm and serene, far very
very far from an indecent forgetful serenity; she has a most
affectionate and tender concern for what has happened. Indeed from the beginning, frightful and hopeless as her disorder seemed, I had confidence enough in her strength of
mind, and religious principle, to look forward to a time
when *even she* might recover tranquillity. God be praised,
Coleridge, wonderful as it is to tell, I have never once been
otherwise than collected, and calm; even on the dreadful
day and in the midst of the terrible scene I preserved a tranquillity, which bystanders may have construed into indifference, a tranquillity not of despair; is it folly or sin in me
to say that it was a religious principle that *most* supported
me? I allow much to other favorable circumstances. I felt
that I had something else to do than to regret; on that first
evening my Aunt was lying insensible, to all appearance like
one dying,—my father, with his poor forehead plaisterd over
from a wound he had received from a daughter dearly loved
by him, and who loved him no less dearly,—my mother a
dead and murder'd corpse in the next room—yet was I won-
derfully supported. I closed not my eyes in sleep that night,
but lay without terrors and without despair. I have lost no
sleep since. I had been long used not to rest in things of
sense, had endeavord after a comprehension of mind, un-
satisfied with the "ignorant present time," and this kept
me up.[12]

The inherent power of such accounts, heightened by a mastery
of language on Charles's part that is stoutly ambiguous or equiv-
ocal about his own complicity and guilt, may well have given
Parker and Evans an unequaled reservoir for a play thoroughly
grounded in authentic circumstances and endless in its impli-
cations.

But they were not alone, and *The Coast of Illyria* was not the
only attempt at the time to recreate the tragedy of Mary Lamb.
There was an intermediate novel by Stephen Southwold (under
the pseudonym of Neil Bell) titled *So Perish the Roses*, published
by Macmillan in New York in 1940, which adds interpretive de-

tail that Parker and Evans incorporate in their play. Where they tend to withhold the inciting incident of *The Coast of Illyria*— the initial moment of shipwreck—to examine its consequences and thereby increase its mystery, its force, and its dread, Bell's narrative is strong and graphically explicit, even when it moves beyond what was then actually known.

On the evening of Wednesday, September the twenty-first, Charles was playing cribbage with his father after supper; Mary was sewing; Aunt Hetty was dozing by the fire; and Mrs. Lamb, downstairs that day for the first time for a week, was reading *Sir Charles Grandison*. Mrs. Brokenshire was out paying a call. Charles, intent on the game and much occupied with his father's pipe, snuff-box and nose, was paying no heed to the others when he was startled by a sharp exclamation from his mother and a cry from Mary, followed immediately by hysterical laughter and incoherent shouting. And then, bursting into tears, Mary hurried from the kitchen and ran upstairs. She returned later, apparently quite calm; and picking up her sewing went on with her work as if unaware of the alarmed and anxious glances directed towards her.

At breakfast next morning she was very quiet, disinclined to talk, and indeed apparently so engrossed with her thoughts that she did not hear the few remarks Charles addressed to her. Much worried by her appearance he called at Dr. Pitcairn's on his way to the office to ask him to go to see Mary during the morning. The doctor was out and not wishing to leave a message on such a matter Charles decided he would go home for his dinner that day, calling in at the doctor's on the way.

Mary was busy in the workroom during the morning, superintending the work of the two apprentices, her manner not noticeably strange. Mrs. Brokenshire, unwell after her evening's entertainment, had remained in bed, and Mary had to share her time between the workroom and the kitchen.

Just before noon she went downstairs to attend to the dinner, taking the younger apprentice, Rosie Bates, with her to lay the table. Her father sat smoking in his big armchair from which he was unable to move without assistance. Her mother and Aunt Hetty sat on opposite sides of the fireplace; Aunt Hetty muttering over her prayer book, which she could no longer see to read; and Mrs. Lamb doing nothing; but plainly in a hypercritical mood, for she was sharply reproving her husband for some delinquency as Mary and Rosie entered.

Rosie presently dropped a spoon and received a stinging reproof from Mrs. Lamb.

"That will do, Mother," Mary said quietly; "please don't interfere."

A moment later Rosie, made clumsy by the watchful eyes of Mrs. Lamb and the general atmosphere of tension, dropped a knife.

"Oh, do be careful, Rosie!" Mary said impatiently.

Rosie mumbled a scared apology, tripped over the curled-up end of the hearthrug, and thrusting out her hand knocked a mug from the table to the floor, where it smashed. Mary uttered a strange, distraught cry and picking up a fork threw it at the sobbing girl. The fork missed the little apprentice and struck Aunt Hetty in the face. The old woman clapped her hand to the wound, cried out, and cowered down in her chair. Mary flung more forks and then snatched up the carving-knife and with a wild cry ran at the child, who darted away screaming, Mary in pursuit round the table. The old man, trembling in his chair, began a frightened whimpering. Mrs. Lamb rose and shouted, "Stop! Mary, stop!" and clutched at her. Mary stopped short, stared at her an instant, and then stabbed her in the breast. Her mother fell back into her chair and as Mary stood stupidly regarding the red blade the door opened and Charles entered. Mary dropped the knife and going over to him put her arms about him and began to cry.

The door from the stairs opened slowly and Mrs. Brokenshire, aroused by the noise, came into the room. Charles silenced her scared enquiries by telling her to go for Dr. Pitcairn, who would be already on his way. Mary dropped to the floor and covered her face with her hands. He went over to his mother and began to unfasten her soaked bodice. She was dead.

When Dr. Pitcairn came he suggested that Mary should be taken to a private madhouse in Islington; and he remained with her while Charles went for a coach, after dispatching Mrs. Brokenshire with a note to the coroner's officer.

Mary was now crouched in a chair. She was no longer crying and seemed unaware of what was happening around her. But before they took her away she said sadly to her brother, "They will send me to Bethlem for life now, Charley." He kissed her, putting her disordered hair back from her face; and then, taking her hands in his, he said gently, "Don't fret, Moll; I will not let them."[13]

Near the end of book 1, Bell introduces another detail to the Lamb story that anticipates the anguished closing of *The Coast of Illyria*.

These emotional orgies [which Charles remembered when he and Mary went on holiday to Widford and he recalled his days there as a young man courting a girl, probably Ann Simmons] led him inevitably towards grosser ones, if only to dull the self-inflicted pain; and he began to sit up long hours after Mary had gone to bed, drinking ale and porter in the bar parlour with the villagers; and later, when the house was closed, making a night of it with solitary swilling of brandy and gin.

His mornings had to pay for his nights and Mary too was made to pay. The pleasant rambles they had enjoyed together the first few days ceased. And the happy talks ceased also, for he was in no mood for conversation until the evening; and then he was quickly too much in the mood and for the sort of half-tipsy facetiousness which Mary disliked and resented.

The holiday ended disastrously, and when but little more than half over. On the Tuesday of their second week Mary showed unmistakable signs of an approaching attack of mental sickness. Alarmed and remorseful, Charles hurried her home. The day after their return the attack developed and threatened to be so serious that Mary, during a lucid period, insisted that she should go back to the Islington madhouse, and at once while she still had possession of her faculties. They set off together, arm-in-arm, to walk there, Mary crying quietly but otherwise composed. They had gone but a few steps along the street when she remembered her straight-jacket and Charles went back for it. As presently he walked along by her side, the straight-jacket under his arm, her hand holding him closely, he felt the windows peopled with those who watched and whispered and pointed, and he began a bitter muttering: "Marked, marked."[14]

Bell's narrative, which recounts Charles's story from his birth to his death, is highly imagistic, and it must therefore have been strongly suggestive to the authors of *The Coast of Illyria* when they were recasting the story for theatrical production.

By contrast, Parker and Evans wrote a well-made play which emulates the classical forms Parker had studied eagerly for five long, hard years at Miss Dana's School in Morristown, New Jersey. The play's central theme concerning Charles and Mary is put openly by Charles to George Dyer in the title passage near the outset of act 3: "Oh, what a couple we are! She in her constant danger, driving me to this; I with my stinking drunkenness sending her quicker to her hells," he remarks. "Two shipwrecked souls. Like 'Twelfth Night,' isn't it? A brother and sister shipwrecked off the coast of Illyria." As it might have happened in a play by Shaw, whom Parker also much admired,[15] this metaphoric shipwreck, whose source is distant, romantic, and *literary*, is translated, like the *Tales from Shakespeare* which brother and sister work at during the play, into their own lives. The figurative is made literal, and the literary real, when George Dyer reports "A harrowing epic. The tale of the ill-fated frigate, 'Favorite.'" It is a story achingly close to Charles's own situation.

There was a ship that lately foundered. It seems that the ship's captain, a man of many voyages, was returning to his native shores with a rich cargo. The heavens had been quite mild when suddenly arose a storm of some fury. The gallant skipper, ever ready to spring to the helm, on his way to that post, stopped in the cabin at the invitation of several com-

mercial gentlemen traveling as passengers. . . . One of the
commercial gentlemen had with him certain bottles of
brandy. It seems that when a bottle had been finished, our
noble sea dog undertook to open a further bottle. While he
was engaged in the task, the ship sank.

Although Charles attempts, somewhat nervously, to laugh the
story off, the shipwreck represents the fortune of East India
House: it is his own fortune, figuratively and literally. After all,
the fortunes of many rest not only on the forces of destiny—
"All the rest of us," that is, the poets, Charles earlier tells Dyer,
"are at sea and sinking"—but result too from the lack of self-
discipline and from the inability to cope with circumstances
that lead them to take refuge in drink or in drugs or in periods of
insanity. A potential cure comes from the other direction—to
distinguish self-serving posturing from inescapably tragic
forces, as Mary herself tells Coleridge in act 2: "Always you mistake the squall for the tempest."

The persistent variations throughout the play on the theme of
a destructive storm and its disastrous results are similar to the
verbal play of Shaw, but the mounting intensity—despite brief
bursts of Parkerian wit which, flashing through various scenes,
only intensify our sense of impending darkness—seems more Ib-
senesque. This carefully structured play emphasizes first a sense
of sailing in the anticipatory exposition of act 1; then images of
sinking in the recognitions that chart act 2; and finally the bru-
tal enlightenment of shipwreck which measures the costs and
compromises of act 3. The use of Hogarth only underscores this
movement—from the cameo of Bedlam on a glass easily broken
in act 1, to a huge painting unavoidable in its confrontation in
act 2, to the world of Hogarth which enters the salon of the
Lambs when Dyer tells of the encroaching greed in a local gin
shop in act 3. Even the opening moments of each act are clues to
its mounting concern: Fanny and Charles open act 1 with joy,
act 2 with signs of strain; but in act 3 at the start Charles is
alone with his battle, and at the close Mary, in her backwards
coat, now a straightjacket against the harsh world, has displaced Fanny for good. And that has been clearly anticipated in
Mary's initial requirement for absolute order and stability—as

Becky has it, "a house without change"—which is succeeded by
her subtle inquiries into the significance of Fanny, and her need
to confront the Hogarth picture of Bedlam as she buries herself
in her rearrangement of Shakespeare. These lead up to her final
delusions: of what Bedlam feels like when she has not yet been
there; of a trip to Cambridge she has forgotten she has taken; of
the historic Mary Blandy, in whom she sees herself when De
Quincey, his own mind in a parallel wandering, drug-induced,
develops the notion of murder as a fine art:

> Some of our murder trials are interminable. Take for ex-
> ample, the case of Mary Blandy. Her trial is the perfect ex-
> ample of what Hamlet calls "the law's delay." Her defenders
> sought for months to excuse her on the ground that she was
> overset in her intellects but—
> (He shrugs)
> I had a friend who was fortunate enough to have seen her
> execution. On the scaffold she said, "Gentlemen, pray do not
> hang me high, for sake of decency." Think of that little light
> body hanging from a rope. Poor little Mary Blandy. Poor
> thing.

Mary Lamb's identification with the "poor thing" is only re-
inforced when Mrs. Crittenden goes further than the law itself
had gone: "She should've been drawn and quartered. She murdered her mother!" In *The Coast of Illyria*, guilt is insistently
complicit, everywhere and nowhere: Mary's final demise can be
laid to genital defect or weakness of mind, but it can also be
laid to Charles's attempt to bring Fanny into a fragile family
situation, to Fanny herself for intruding, to Coleridge for belit-
tling Mary's illness and for his own prattling, to Hazlitt's igno-
rance and De Quincey's coarseness; to Mrs. Crittenden: when
something is so delicate as a sensitive and artistic mind, who is
to judge the efficient agent that threatens and destroys it?
    The play's treatment of the central private and public problem
of a sensitive woman like Mary Lamb is akin to the drama of
Ibsen, but the theatrical properties and images resemble those
of a third playwright whom Parker emulated, Chekhov. The
various props—the laudanum pipe, the portrait of a kneeling
girl with a lamb and a spray of roses, the shepherd and shepherd-

ess figurines, the Hogarth glasses and pictures—and both the knives—the letter opener and the bread knife—underscore the play's tension as well as its intention. So do actions, such as Coleridge's emerging with Charles's essay "Confessions of a Drunkard" obviously protruding from his pocket or his recitation of "Kubla Khan" with its own visionary beauty and madness intertwined. Nearly all of these objects and scenes—the laudanum, the portrait of the girl, the Hogarth pictures, the letter opener, the "Confessions," the delivery of "Kubla Khan"—are historical incidents Parker and Evans researched, but their selection and arrangement, deliberate and exacting, are what make *The Coast of Illyria* the "pretty damn powerful play" Romola Robb remembers.

"I'd like to do a play more than anything," Parker told Marion Capron in an interview for the *Paris Review*; "First night is the most exciting thing in the world. It's wonderful to hear your words spoken."[16] Very early in her career, she reviewed drama—for *Vanity Fair*, for *Ainslee's*, for the *New Yorker*—but she also occasionally tried her hand at writing for the theater. Her first attempt was modest—a song performed by Robert Sherwood in *No, Siree!*, a revue staged by the Algonquin wits in April 1922; the revue was later rewritten by Parker and Robert Benchley as a one-act play, *Nero*, which ran to half-empty houses for fifteen performances in November. (A final contribution to Broadway was also a single lyric for the 1956 Leonard Bernstein–Lillian Hellman version of *Candide*.) In 1923 she joined George S. Kaufman and Marc Connelly in writing a sketch for a similar revue, *'Round the Town*.

Parker's first full-length play was written with Elmer Rice; according to Marion Meade, Parker did "practically all the writing while Rice concentrated on scene construction and plot development."[17] Originally called *Soft Music*, it was later retitled *Close Harmony; or, The Lady Next Door*. The show began a pre-opening run in Wilmington, Delaware, on November 22, 1924, before opening on Broadway on December 1. *Close Harmony* is a slight domestic drama, adequate for its time, which is succinctly summarized by Benchley in his review for the old *Life* magazine.

A poor little guy who is "happily married," except for the fact that he is miserable, meets a neighbor's wife who isn't even "happily married." They find that they have something in common. She plays the piano and he plays the mandolin—when his wife will let him. They get together one afternoon and he picks out "The Blue Danube" to her accompaniment and, inflamed by the nominal success of this, they sing "The Sunshine of Your Smile" together. The delicate writing of this scene, combined with the practically perfect work of James Spottswood and Wanda Lyon, makes it just about as heartbreaking a thing as we have ever seen on the stage.[18]

Heywood Broun agreed in the *Sunday World*: "The scene at the piano and round about is the most authentic and interesting combination of actuality and theatrical effectiveness which I have seen this year."[19] The difficulty, however, is that the play seems to be written largely for this single scene.

The situation bears strong resemblance to Parker's first story, "Such a Pretty Little Picture," which also examines a man trapped in an unhappy marriage who outwardly conforms but inwardly rebels. *Close Harmony* reveals such frustration by showing certain surface similarities between Ed Graham, a suburbanite with a nagging wife and a self-centered, critical daughter ironically named "Sister," and Belle Sheridan, Sister's piano teacher and a former burlesque star whose husband, now out of work, spends his time in the City with other women. Their Saturday afternoon meeting, during which they show sympathy for each other, leads to a show of mutual affection followed by plans for an elopement. But Sister is hit in the stomach at a children's birthday party and Ed is confronted with family responsibilities he cannot bring himself to leave. Belle understands, although she plans to leave her husband anyway. "I hate to leave you here, Ed. But it's all right, I guess. Look— I'm the way I am—and you're your way—and Bert's his—I guess we're all better off where we belong. You see, don't you?"[20] He does, but the magic of their hours together, which gave her the strength to leave Bert, gives Ed renewed strength within his home. He sends his visiting sister-in-law back to New Bedford, tells his daughter to stop complaining, and instructs his wife to

prepare eggs for dinner since he burned the roast while distracted with Belle. Then Ed takes down his mandolin. But he
does not play it long; "*After about eight bars he gradually leaves
off playing, takes the pipe from his mouth and looks out into
space as* THE [final] CURTAIN FALLS."[21]
Close Harmony is consciously a well-made play. The domestic
quarrel of act 1 is paralleled in act 2 and given joint resolution
in act 3; the play has a careful and economic management of a
small cast; and Belle's living room, in act 2, is a cheapened version of Ed's home in acts 1 and 3, since both houses are part of
the same building development. But Parker and Rice make triv-
iality their chief means of exposing the limited mediocrity of
their characters, and so the characters, like their lines, tend to
be clichéd and predictable. If Ed has any insights worth record-
ing, they are caught only in pantomime as the curtain falls, and
so are insufficiently rendered. "It was dull," Parker said on several later occasions; "you have my apologies."[22] The play ran for
twenty-four performances before it closed, quietly, near the end
of the month in which it began.

   In 1939 Parker returned to playwriting, this time adapting a
comedy by the Hungarian writer Miklos Laxzlo with her husband, Alan Campbell. But *The Happiest Man* is, in the end,
largely an original work. It centers on a man who works for a
plumbing supply company and who is suddenly fired after eigh-
teen years of labor. Unlike *Close Harmony*, which combines wit
with pathos, here humor uneasily accompanies polemics. Plans
called for Otto Preminger to direct and for Paul Muni and Bur-
gess Meredith to play the major roles, but the producer, Max
Gordon, dropped his option with no reason and Parker and
Campbell were unable to get the play staged.

   The Ladies of the Corridor, which was written with Arnaud
d'Usseau and which opened at the Longacres Theatre in New
York on October 21, 1953, was another matter entirely; it was
"the only thing I ever did I was proud of," she told Richard Lamparski in a radio interview more than a decade later.[23] D'Usseau
still remembers their daily day-long sessions (with a lunch
break) of working seriously on the play in a residential hotel
where Parker lived until she moved, during the course of
composition, to the Volney. The idea for the play had been
d'Usseau's; he knew of older women whose lives seemed empty

and aimless when their husbands died. Parker added her own observations of aging single women and widows in hotels like the Volney. "We worked hard," d'Usseau recalls; with d'Usseau's support, Parker even stopped drinking when she was working, for her work was crucial and took all her attention and energy. Parker and d'Usseau wrote each scene, each line, together. Somewhere, he recalls, Willa Cather's *A Lost Lady* had its effects during the formative stages; and a number of characters in the play bear striking resemblances to moments in Cather's brief novel. Lulu Ames (who was played by Edna Best) is anticipated in the Mrs. Forrester Niel Herbert sees when he returns to Sweet Water in part 2:

> She showed no impatience to be released [from his much younger arms], but lay laughing up at him with that gleam of something elegantly wild, something fantastic and tantalizing,—seemingly so artless, really the most finished artifice! She put her hand under his chin as if he were still a boy.
>
> "And how handsome he's grown! Isn't the old Judge proud of you! He called me up last night and began sputtering, 'It's only fair to warn you, Ma'm, that I've a very handsome boy over here.' As if I hadn't known you would be! And now you're a man, and have seen the world! Well, what have you found in it?"[24]

Mildred Tynan (Betty Field) is drawn from Mrs. Forrester at a later stage, when alcoholism helps her to accommodate loneliness and age.

> As the women came and went through the lane, Niel sometimes overheard snatches of their conversation. . . .
> "There are nine dozen glasses," said Molly Tucker, "counting them for beer and whiskey. If there is a sale, I've a mind to bid on a couple of them green ones, with long stems, for mantel ornaments. But she'll never sell 'em all, unless she can get the saloons to take 'em."
> Ed Elliott's mother laughed. "She'll never sell 'em, as long as she's got anything to put in 'em."
> "The cellar will go dry, some day."
> "I guess there's always plenty that will get it for such as

her. I never go there now that I don't smell it on her. I went over late the other night, and she was on her knees, washing up the kitchen floor. Her eyes were glassy. She kept washing the place around the ice-box over and over, till it made me nervous. I said, 'Mrs. Forrester, I think you've washed that place several times already.'"

"Was she confused?"

"Not a particle! She laughed and said she was often absent-minded." [25]

At still a later stage, Mrs. Forrester's portrait has hints of Parker's Constance Mercer (Margaret Barker): "'[S]he's after the young ones,' said Ed Elliott's mother. 'She's getting childish.'" [26] But Mrs. Forrester can rationalize one-night stands and younger men to the younger Niel.

She looked at him with pleading plausibility. "I am getting rested after a long strain. And while I wait, I'm finding new friends among the young men,—those your age, and a little younger. I've wanted for a long while to do something for the boys in this town, but my hands were full. I hate to see them growing up like savages, when all they need is a civilized house to come to, and a woman to give them a few hints. They've never had a chance. You wouldn't be the boy you are if you'd never gone to Boston,—and you've always had older friends who'd seen better days. Suppose you had grown up like Ed Elliott and Joe Simpson?" [27]

Like nearly everything Parker wrote, *The Ladies of the Corridor* deals with abandonment—both the individual abandonment of Mildred by her ambitious and selfish husband and of Lulu Ames by the young man she hopes will save her from a prolonged widowhood at the age of fifty and the public abandonment of senior citizens by a world that places a considerably higher premium on youth.

The aging Lulu, whose husband has been dead only a short time, feels these conditions most acutely.

I don't know how to get myself fixed up. There's something lacking. I guess there's something lacking in a lot of women; nobody's ever one of a kind. We were told you grew up, you got married, and there you were. And so we did, and so there we were. But our husbands, they were busy. We weren't part of their lives; and as we got older we weren't part of anybody's lives, and yet we never learned how to be alone. It's different with girls now. But that's the way it was with me.[28]

The younger, more hardened Mildred sees the other women in her hotel with a derision that etches her own sense of worthlessness.

Those old hags in the corridor. (*She raises her glass*) Well, here's to them. There they are: money they've got—nothing to worry about they've got—twenty years of life they've got. And for what? Just to sit there. Vegetables they are, sitting there in their bins, waiting for the garbage collector to come and get them.[29]

The middle-aged, successful businesswoman, Connie, sees through them. When her longtime friend Lulu is invited to go to the movies with the older residents, Connie warns her against it: "Don't you do it. Those women are dead, and death is contagious."[30]

Eric Bentley's comments on the play acknowledge both the larger social issues Parker and d'Usseau meant to expose and the specific case studies which became their chief method. *The Ladies of the Corridor*, Bentley writes,

is a story about the derelict women who live in hotels. A young one, who has a husband that uses a whip and keeps the company of call girls, takes to drink, disgusts herself by sleeping with the desk clerk, and commits suicide. An old one, concealing behind her old lace the arsenic of maternal tyranny, forces her son into spending his life with her by threatening to expose the fact that he had given up his last job under suspicion of homosexuality. A middle-aged one has a pathetic love affair with a younger man. As a kind of chorus commenting on the three principals, there is, on the one side, a successful career woman and, on the other, a couple of hags whose life is death.[31]

For Parker, the play's theme is the "appalling human waste" and the setting of the Hotel Marlowe a microcosm of the larger American society.

"We're trying to show a part of American life—and a very large part of it," she said. "There is an enormous population of women alone. . . . It's not so much age as manlessness—and they should be better trained, adjusted, to live a life without a man.

"I think in many cases they're contented women; they wouldn't change places with anyone, and if you possibly told any of them they were miserably unhappy, they'd think you were insane. But some of them don't know they're dead—that curious death in life with which they are content. . . . It sounds too pompous, I know. . . . but I don't think tragedy is too big a word because the waste is unnecessary."[32]

There is more wit in *Ladies of the Corridor* than in *Coast of Illyria*—d'Usseau has commented on the need for it[33]—but it is a mordant humor, self-directed, the cruel and rueful jokes among the aging women displaying a last shared personal and psychic stay against the terror of emptiness. If it seems a meager response, it is a tactic which has for them grown from deeply embedded self-awareness, now hoary with age but no less authentic and no less vital.

The title of *The Ladies of the Corridor*, like that of *The Coast of Illyria*, stems from a literary allusion, this time to lines from T. S. Eliot's "Sweeney Erect":

> The ladies of the corridor
> Find themselves involved, disgraced,
> Call witness to their principles
> And deprecate the lack of taste.

The setting, the Hotel Marlowe in the East Sixties, is a composite of residential hotels in mid-Manhattan and, in the play, the crossroads of the world. In the lobby sit as a Greek chorus two of the derelicts, Mrs. Gordon and Mrs. Lauterbach, whose running comments provide bankrupt social judgments and deathlike interpretations, *thanatos* embodied and so verified. Mrs. Gordon's tag—"Well, what's new on the Rialto?" (apparently unconsciously derived from *The Merchant of Venice*)—is at once an attempt to be witty and a metaphor to suggest that if all the world's a stage, here the stage is meant to be all the world. She is the most theatrical, the most artificial (she frequently changes her nail polish), for her life is altogether vicarious: she lives the lives of hotel residents by day and the lives of movie actors by night. Her kleptomania—she steals a blue ashtray from Mrs. Lauterbach and some of Mildred's cards after Mildred commits suicide—suggests her fundamentally parasitic nature. Mrs. Lauterbach's more pathetic loneliness—she wants to see her son at Thanksgiving, but he hasn't invited her and she is afraid that if she writes him it will seem like "pushing"—is ignored by Mrs. Gordon, blind to compassion. Because of the coldness of the one, and the warmth of the other, their relationship is peculiarly unrewarding, infertile.

Others seem to hold out more promise. Mrs. Nichols has adjusted to life by using her son, Charles: she manages their affairs through investments and joins her son in stamp collecting (another allusion to the Marlowe as a microcosm). Charles Nichols, whose chief occupation is "Gray Lady," a nurse companion to his mother, spends each day at the zoo. His mother forces the significance of this on him.

> All [the animals] in their nice clean cages, nice and warm?
> . . . Poor caged things. And yet they say that when one of
> them escapes he's frightened out of his wits. He doesn't know
> what to do. Why is that, Charlie? . . . Too much soft living, I
> expect. And too much care—yes, and affection. I've always
> heard the keepers are extremely fond of them.[34]

Such an obvious analogy does not go unnoticed by Charles, who fully understands the monstrosity and viciousness of her emotional blackmail (a point Brooks Atkinson and other reviewers missed).

Just as Mrs. Nichols first appears a gentle and well-bred woman, Mildred seems at first a typed dipsomaniac. Drink, she tells the maid Irma, "makes you a different person. You're not yourself for a little while, and that's velvet. . . . A couple of drinks, and I've got some nerve. Otherwise I'm frightened all the time."[35] But she has a desperate kind of wit—"I'm giving up solitaire. I can't win even when I cheat" and "Maybe I could give music lessons to backward children. . . . I finally got so I could play the 'Minute Waltz' in a minute and a half"[36]—that shows how frightened she remains even after she has been drinking. For the drinking is a consequence not of fear in the present but of searing memories from the past with her husband.

Once I got started—God, how he hurried me along. So when we went to the country club, Mrs. John Tynan would fall down on the dance floor and her husband would carry her out. And everybody would say, "Oh, that poor man, and look how sweet he is to her! Poor, dear man." Holy John Tynan, the Blessed Martyr of Santa Barbara. Yes, and the call girls, two and three at a time, and the whip in the closet.[37]

As then, hers is still a life of lies, and her hope in finding a new job at Irma's suggestion, like the hope in the bottle and in the driven affair with the bellhop Harry, is futile. She knows that pretense is her life—and that her life is pretense. Her suicide is superbly plotted, and her last line—a wisecrack—illuminates her utter despondency.

The chief character in *Ladies of the Corridor* is Lulu Ames, who upon the death of her husband in Akron moves to this crossroads to begin a new life near a son and daughter-in-law who do not really want her so close. Her friend Connie tells her how to cope.

Lulu: Is there a man, Connie?
Connie: No; oh, no. After Ben died there was a long stretch when I sat and looked at the wall. Then, a long time after that, there was a man—a lovely man. I was young again.
Lulu (Gently): What happened, Connie?
Connie: He found somebody who was young for the first time. So then there was a succession of transients. If that shocks you, Lulu, it shouldn't. The one-night stands don't do any good; I found that out. There's got to be fondness, and there's got to be hope. Lulu, please—this new life must be all you want it to be. Only don't let yourself get lonely. Loneliness makes ladies our age do the goddamnedest things.[38]

Lulu finds a young man whose solitude after the breakup of his marriage mirrors her own. For a while, their relationship is tender and successful; but Lulu does not want to attend young people's parties with Paul, and as they grow more distant, she

grows increasingly anxious about losing him. "Look, Lulu,"
Paul replies, "two people, no matter what their feeling, mustn't
feed entirely on each other . . . If they do, all that's left of them
is a little heap of bones."[39] His comment is true for them, for
Mrs. Nichols and Charles, and for the women in the lobby. But
like the others, Lulu cannot help herself, and the relationship
collapses "because the sweetness has gone out of it—the loveliness."[40] The paradigmatic relationship of Lulu and Paul anticipates Mildred's death in the next scene, for her actual suicide is
only a more visible form of the spiritual suicide shared by all
the others.

The Ladies of the Corridor, like Parker's other plays, is classi-
cally formed: the published script has two acts of six scenes
each, many of them parallel, and the overall work is enclosed
by the chorus in the lobby. The sharp episodic structure, moreover, enables Parker and d'Usseau to heighten and dramatize
what in longer, more traditional scenes would be humdrum
lives. But when the play opened in Philadelphia it ran until
12:30 A.M.—far too long—and Parker and d'Usseau set to work
rearranging and cutting scenes. As a result, there are now in the
archives three versions of the play—the original typescript of
150 pages, a shortened version of 134 pages, and the published
text, with some 119 textual changes between the first and final
drafts (given in part here at the end of this volume). Most
changes were made in the scene where Lulu and Paul part, but
Irma's role is condensed and made less sympathetic while other
abridgments remove Mrs. Gordon's mendacity, Connie's promo-
tion, Paul's praise of Lulu, and Lulu's rationale for not meeting
Paul's friends. Harold Clurman, who staged the play, also insisted on changing the ending to something more ambiguous
and hopeful, a change to which d'Usseau agreed since it allows
the play to ask more questions. Parker, however, objected. "I
vehemently protested, but who was I against so many?" she told
Richard Lamparski. In the original script, Lulu becomes "a lady
of the corridor herself. That was the whole point of the play, but
instead she found a way to live and work." Parker knew that
that is not what happened to those women; her original version
"was a bitter play, but true."[41] Many critics, however, received
the new version warmly, and George Jean Nathan named The

Ladies of the Corridor the best play of the year. Although it ran for only forty-five performances, it has recently been adapted for public television by d'Usseau; the new production stars Cloris Leachman as Lulu, Mike Farrell as Paul, and Jane Wyatt as Mrs. Nichols and has again been very successful. This slightly shortened version—the fourth—retains the possibility that Lulu, who has surrendered to a life of needlework, may still keep her equilibrium and survive. "There is one thing worse than loneliness," she tells Mrs. Gordon and Mrs. Lauterbach at the close, "and that is the fear of it."

The Ladies of the Corridor remains one of Parker's finest works, and within a year she and d'Usseau were collaborating on another play, *The Ice Age*. This study of a homosexual relationship was "daring," d'Usseau recalls, and "ahead of its time." [42] A young, tanned tennis player who is newly married, Gordon Corey, is hired by Adrian Zabel, the director of a New York museum, as his assistant, although Gordon has no experience or particular talent for the position. Slowly their relationship, initiated by Adrian, develops. At the same time, Gordon's marriage to Daisy deteriorates despite their escape from living with his overbearing mother—a putative cause of his homosexual tendencies—and the birth of their first child. Gordon desultorily fights his homosexual tendencies and at one point tries unsuccessfully to leave Adrian, but the older man's fine hands, fine tastes, and wealth prove irresistible. As with another relationship to a former employee, Bob Matthews (who was abandoned and fired by Adrian, turns alcoholic, and later in the play commits suicide), Adrian is demanding although ultimately cold and unsympathetic; from the start he is dominant and tyrannical. The young photographer Don attempts to tell Gordon this: "Mr. Z. is a cold baby. You've heard him called the 'iceberg' around here," and when Gordon denies that, Don continues,

No, I suppose you haven't, at that. You're his assistant here. Sundays you play tennis with him. You're in. You're close. Nobody's going to say anything about him to you. An iceberg is what he is. The part you see is great—all white and glistening in the sun. But the submerged part—the two thirds—that's what kills. [43]

Adrian's coldness does kill Bob Matthews, and Don's description is confirmed when Don reports Bob's death to Adrian.

> His life was a mess. Now his death is. That's all. I suggest
> you have him cremated.
>   (Goes to his desk)
> May I contribute a check?
>   (Takes out a check book)
> Perhaps you think I should have done this while he was
> alive. If I had once given him money, he would have got his
> foot in the door.
>   (Writes a check)
> I'm not doing this out of charity, Don. I've never subscribed
> to the preposterous theory that I'm my brother's keeper. I'm
> doing it only to save face in front of you. For myself, I'd let
> the City take care of him. Let him go down the river with
> the garbage.
>   (Gives Don the check)
> Here you are. I've made it out to cash.[44]

When Gordon at last realizes the total impact of his own commitment to Adrian, he attacks him and apparently kills him.

Like other plays on which Parker collaborated, *The Ice Age* is a well-made work. The two scenes of act 1 contrast Adrian's warm interview with Gordon and the cold home in which Gordon and Daisy are required to live with Mrs. Corey. The other two acts are parallel. They are divided into three scenes: in each we move from Adrian's office, where he confronts Gordon in act 2 and wins his devotion in act 3; to Gordon's new walk-up with Daisy, where Gordon feels a kind of awkwardness and emptiness; to Adrian's apartment above the museum, where the seductions in both acts occur. There are the theatrical touches we have come to expect, too. Gordon strips at one point to suntan onstage; later Adrian presents him with an exquisite mirror which he will later break in self-disgust and self-repulsion. But on the whole, the characters need more motivation and more development and the plot more subtlety. Parker and d'Usseau realized this too, for the play was never completed; the sole extant copy is missing the final pages.

P arker's two collaborations with Arnaud d'Usseau came after her work on *The Coast of Illyria*, for which, true to form, she had also found a coauthor. He was Rosser Lynn Evans, twenty years her junior, a handsome, well-built man, whom Parker first met in 1942 in Miami, where he was in the U.S. Army Air Corps with Alan Campbell. Meade notes that Evans was already suffering from alcoholism, as did Parker's husbands, Edwin Pond Parker and Campbell.[45] After the war, Parker met Evans again in New York City, where he was a radio announcer. She suggested that the two of them collaborate on a play about Charles and Mary Lamb, and Evans moved in with her. They worked on a story, "The Game," for *Cosmopolitan* magazine and then, in Hollywood, on *The Fan*, a film version of Oscar Wilde's play *Lady Windermere's Fan*, for Otto Preminger. Evans had been married, had written two unsuccessful novels, and had had three off-Broadway plays produced before he began writing filmscripts. J. Bryan III describes him as "a pleasant, shambling, hobbledehoy with huge, lump-toed Army boots that instantly inspired our children to call him 'Li'l Abner,' in tribute to Al Capp's lamented naif, Abner Yokum."[46] Evans continued not only as Parker's collaborator but as her companion; in turn, she paid his bills and gave him whatever he wanted.

The Coast of Illyria reads mostly like other works that Parker wrote herself. At the rehearsals in Dallas, cast and crew members recall that Evans said very little, although he helped Parker with revisions. She gave him primary credit for helping her research the play and for going to the library for the countless books which she said she consulted. The two of them remained in Dallas for part of the first week's run and then returned to their residence in the Chateau Marmont on Sunset Boulevard in Hollywood. A short time later they decided to take a brief vacation in Mexico, where they quarreled and permanently separated.

If fetching books was Evans's primary function, he nevertheless contributed a great deal, for much of *The Coast of Illyria* is taken, sometimes verbatim, from the letters and essays of Charles and Mary Lamb, the letters of Coleridge, selected essays of

Hazlitt and De Quincey, and De Quincey's *Confessions of an English Opium Eater*. Additional ideas and even inspiration must also have come from the popular books on the Lambs that appeared with rather remarkable concentration in the United States in the early 1940s. E. V. Lucas's edition of the works of Charles and Mary Lamb was published in 1903 and was followed by his definitive *Life of Charles Lamb* in 1905 and *The Letters* in 1935. Edmund Blunden used many of these documents in his Cambridge lectures, which were collected in *Charles Lamb and His Contemporaries* and published by the university in 1933, and for the excerpts he assembled in 1934 for the Hogarth Press. In the United States, interest in the Lambs grew quickly with the publication of Neil Bell's novel *So Perish the Roses* and Ernest C. Ross's more scholarly study *The Ordeal of Bridget Elia* (Charles's name for Mary in the *Essays of Elia*), published by the University of Oklahoma Press, both of which appeared in 1940. Two other books, even more popular, followed: Will D. Howe's *Charles Lamb and His Friends* from Bobbs-Merrill in 1944 and Katharine Anthony's *The Lambs* from Knopf in 1945.

These more recent books are where Parker, with Evans's help, seems to have begun. She took from Katharine Anthony the picture of the girl with the lamb and roses (a picture that fascinated Mary as a child), the connection between Mary Lamb and Mary Blandy, Mary's preoccupation with thoughts of Bedlam (where in fact she never went), Coleridge's anxiety over Wordsworth's treatment of him, and some fundamental characteristics of Dyer, Becky (the spelling of the name is Anthony's), and Emma. In Howe's study, Parker found a description of Charles's alcoholism attributed to Thomas Carlyle, an account of Dyer's forgetfulness that is used in the play, an account of Charles's pension from East India House (which Parker transforms), and the anecdote concerning the hapless Tommy Blye, whose salary is cut to one-sixth of its original sum because of his tardiness and irresponsibility, an analogy that weighs on Charles in *The Coast of Illyria*. In addition, Parker read Ernest Ross's useful character sketches of Mary, Mrs. Lamb, Coleridge, Becky, Emma, Fanny Kelly, and Dyer, as well as detailed accounts of a trip Charles and Mary Lamb made to Cambridge in 1815 (the source of Mary's hallucination in act 3), of the Wednesday (previously Thursday) nights at the Lambs, and of the concern Charles felt over yet another shipwreck, that of the East India ship *Earl of Abergavenny*, which sank off Portland Bill on February 5, 1805, with Wordsworth's brother John as its captain. The description Parker found here of Mary Lamb, drawn from the Lambs' friend Charles Cowden Clarke, was especially helpful.

> Miss Lamb bore a strong personal resemblance to her brother; being in stature under middle height, possessing well-cut features, and a countenance of singular sweetness, with intelligence. Her brown eyes were soft, yet penetrating; her nose and mouth very shapely; while the general expression was mildness itself. She had a speaking-voice, gentle and persuasive. . . . She had a mind at once nobly-toned and practical, making her ever a chosen source of confidence among her friends, who turned to her for consolation, confirmation, and advice.[47]

Ross's sketch of Dyer was also useful: "He was near-sighted and absent-minded, humorless and as guileless as a child. He wrote good prose but poor verse; in fact, he had the common failing of not being able to distinguish verse from poetry. But he was a lovable character."[48]

But the language of *The Coast of Illyria* shows signs everywhere that Parker also immersed herself in Lamb's own writings so as to get the period right. One of the most remarkable accomplishments of the play, in fact, is the ability of Parker and Evans to sustain echoes of Charles and Mary even when they are not quoting or paraphrasing them. There is, for instance, Charles's letter to Dorothy Wordsworth on June 14, 1805:

> Your long, kind letter has not been thrown away (for it has given me great pleasure to find you are all resuming your old occupations, and are better); but poor Mary to whom it is address't, cannot yet relish it. She has been attacked by one of her severe illnesses, and is at present *from home*. Last Monday week was the day she left me; and I hope I may

calculate upon having her again in a month, or little more. I
am rather afraid late hours have in this case contributed to
her indisposition. . . . I have every reason to suppose that
this illness, like all her former ones, will be but temporary;
but I cannot always feel so. Meantime she is dead to me, and
I miss a prop. All my strength is gone, and I am like a [fool,
ber]eft of her co-operation. I dare not think, lest I [should
think] wrong; so used am I to look up to her [in the least]
and the biggest perplexity. To say *all that* [I know of her]
would be more than I think any body could [believe or even
under]stand; and when I hope to have her well [again with
me] it would be sinning against her feelings to go about to
praise her; for I can conceal nothing that I do from her. She
is older, and wiser, and better, than me, and all my
wretched imperfections I cover to myself by resolutely thinking on her goodness. She would share life and death, heaven
and hell, with me. She lives but for me. And I know I have
been wasting and teazing her life for five years past inces-
santly with my cursed drinking and ways of going on. But
even in the up-braiding of myself I am offending against her,
for I know that she has cleaved to me for better, for worse;
and if the balance has been against her hitherto, it was a
noble trade.[49]

This is the aloneness we find at the beginning of act 1 of *The
Coast of Illyria*, when Charles describes his feelings not to Dorothy Wordsworth but to Fanny Kelly. They combine the sentiment of his 1797 Christmas Day poem to the absent Mary—

> I am a widow'd thing, now thou art gone!
> Now thou art gone, my own familiar friend,
> Companion, sister, help-mate, counsellor!
> Alas! that honour'd mind, whose sweet reproof
> And meekest wisdom in times past have smooth'd
> The unfilial harshness of my foolish speech,
> And made me loving to my parents old,
> (Why is this so, ah God! why is this so?)
> That honour'd mind become a fearful blank,
> Her senses lock'd up, and herself kept out
> From human sight or converse, while so many

> Of the foolish sort are left to roam at large,
> Doing all acts of folly, and sin, and shame?
> Thy paths are mystery![50]

—with the rueful shame of his alcoholism. His "Confessions of
a Drunkard" first appeared in the *Philanthropist* in September
1813 but was frequently reprinted. It is the basis for the portrait
of Charles at the opening of act 3 of *The Coast of Illyria*.

> I have known one in that state, when he has tried to ab-
> stain but for one evening,—though the poisonous potion had
> long ceased to bring back its first enchantments, though he
> was sure it would rather deepen his gloom than brighten
> it,—in the violence of the struggle, and the necessity he has
> felt of getting rid of the present sensation at any rate, I have
> known him to scream out, to cry aloud, for the anguish and
> pain of the strife within him.
> Why should I hesitate to declare, that the man of whom I
> speak is myself? . . .
> To be an object of compassion to friends, of derision to
> foes; to be suspected by strangers, stared at by fools; to be
> esteemed dull when you cannot be witty, to be applauded
> for witty when you know that you have been dull; to be
> called upon for the extemporaneous exercise of that faculty
> which no premeditation can give; to be spurred on to efforts
> which end in contempt; to be set on to provoke mirth which
> procures the procurer hatred; to give pleasure and be paid
> with squinting malice; to swallow draughts of life-destroying
> wine which are to be distilled into airy breath to tickle vain
> auditors; to mortgage miserable morrows for nights of mad-
> ness; to waste whole seas of time upon those who pay it back
> in little inconsiderable drops of grudging applause,—are the
> wages of buffoonery and death. . . .
> I perpetually catch myself in tears, for any cause, or none.
> It is inexpressible how much this infirmity adds to a sense of
> shame, and a general feeling of deterioration.[51]

But while Charles openly refers to his alcoholism and to Mary's
illnesses, he refrains from discussing his own early mental illness
or the family's theory that a tendency toward mental illness was
derived from his father's side.

Many of Charles's most charming *Essays of Elia* and *Last Essays of Elia* are based on his life with Mary and with other close companions. "Mackery End, in Hertfordshire" was frequently cited in Parker's and Evans's sources for its description of what would become the situation for *The Coast of Illyria*.

> Bridget Elia has been my housekeeper for many a long year. I have obligations to Bridget, extending beyond the period of memory. We house together, old bachelor and maid, in a sort of double singleness; with such tolerable comfort, upon the whole, that I, for one, find in myself no sort of disposition to go out upon the mountains, with the rash king's offspring, to bewail my celibacy. We agree pretty well in our tastes and habits—yet so, as "with a difference." We are generally in harmony, with occasional bickerings—as it should be among near relations. Our sympathies are rather understood, than expressed; and once, upon my dissembling a tone in my voice more kind than ordinary, my cousin burst into tears, and complained that I was altered. We are both great readers in different directions. While I am hanging over (for the thousandth time) some passage in old Burton, or one of his strange contemporaries, she is abstracted in some modern tale, or adventure, whereof our common reading-table is daily fed with assiduously fresh supplies. . . .
>
> We are both of us inclined to be a little too positive; and I have observed the result of our disputes to be almost uniformly this—that in matters of fact, dates, and circumstances, it turns out, that I was in the right, and my cousin in the wrong. But where we have differed upon moral points; upon something proper to be done, or let alone; whatever heat of opposition, or steadiness of conviction, I set out with, I am sure always, in the long run, to be brought over to her way of thinking.[52]

In "The Superannuated Man," which appeared in *Last Essays of Elia*, Charles discusses his retirement. It came much later than it does in the play—after thirty-six years of service, when he was fifty—and it occurred when he was summoned to the office one day at work, but the pension and purpose were the same and so was Charles's surprise and immense joy.

On the evening of the 12th of April, just as I was about quit-
ting my desk to go home (it might be about eight o'clock) I
received an awful summons to attend the presence of the
whole assembled firm in the formidable back parlour. I
thought, now my time is surely come, I have done for myself, I am going to be told that they have no longer occasion
for me. L——, I could see, smiled at the terror I was in,
which was a little relief to me,—when to my utter astonish-
ment B——, the eldest partner, began a formal harangue to
me on the length of my services, my very meritorious conduct during the whole of the time (the deuce, thought I,
how did he find out that? I protest I never had the confidence
to think as much). He went on to descant on the expediency
of retiring at a certain time of life (how my heart panted!)
and asking me a few questions as to the amount of my own
property, of which I have a little, ended with a proposal, to
which his three partners nodded a grave assent, that I should
accept from the house, which I had served so well, a pension
for life to the amount of two-thirds of my accustomed salary—a magnificent offer! I do not know what I answered between surprise and gratitude, but it was understood that I
accepted their proposal, and I was told that I was free from
that hour to leave their service.[53]

Mr. Wilberforce is the playwrights' invention. They have taken
the anxiety and pleasure of this moment and transferred it instead to their invented version of Charles's proposal to Fanny;
historically, he made a rather oblique proposal to her by letter
which she declined in a written response a few hours later.

Others of Lamb's essays clearly influenced the conception of
The Coast of Illyria. "On the Genius and Character of Hogarth"
tells why Charles and Mary collected the series of *A Rake's
Progress*, which hung in what became known as their "print
room," and suggests that historically both of them lived with
those stark pictures constantly. In his essay Charles is explicit
about why Hogarth appealed to him.

In the scene in Bedlam, which terminates the *Rake's Progress*, we find the same assortment of the ludicrous with the
terrible. Here is desperate madness, the overturning of origi-

nally strong thinking faculties, at which we shudder, as we
contemplate the duration and pressure of affliction which it
must have asked to destroy such a building;—and here is the
gradual hurtless lapse into idiocy, of faculties, which at their
best of times never having been strong, we look upon the
consummation of their decay with no more pity than is consistent with a smile. The mad taylor, the poor driveller that
has gone out of his wits (and truly he appears to have had
no great journey to go to get past their confines) for the love
of *Charming Betty Careless*,—these half-laughable, scarce-
pitiable objects take off from the horror which the principal
figure would of itself raise, at the same time that they assist
the feeling of the scene by contributing to the general notion
of its subject:—

> Madness, thou chaos of the brain,
> What art, that pleasure giv'st, and pain?
> Tyranny of Fancy's reign!
> Mechanic Fancy, that can build
> Vast labyrinths and mazes wild,
> With rule disjointed, shapeless measure,
> Fill'd with horror, fill'd with pleasure!
> Shapes of horror, that would even
> Cast doubts of mercy upon heaven.
> Shapes of pleasure, that, but seen,
> Would split the shaking sides of spleen. . . .

[The Madman in the Bedlam scene] is the stretch of human
suffering to the utmost endurance, severe bodily pain
brought on by strong mental agony, the frightful obstinate
laugh of madness,—yet all so unforced and natural, that
those who never were witness to madness in real life, think
they see nothing but what is familiar to them in this face.
Here are no tricks of distortion, nothing but the natural face
of agony. This is high tragic painting.[54]

Charles's persistent concern about the relationship between
sanity and the art of genius is clear from his essay "Sanity of
True Genius," in which the claims made for the artist are stout
and positive.

So far from the position holding true, that great wit (or
genius, in our modern way of speaking), has a necessary al-

liance with insanity, the greatest wits, on the contrary, will ever be found to be the sanest writers. It is impossible for the mind to conceive of a mad Shakspeare. The greatness of wit, by which the poetic talent is here chiefly to be understood, manifests itself in the admirable balance of all the faculties. Madness is the disproportionate straining or excess of any one of them. "So strong a wit," says Cowley, speaking of a poetical friend,

>   "——did Nature to him frame,
>   As all things but his judgment overcame,
>   His judgment like the heavenly moon did show,
>   Tempering that mighty sea below."

The ground of the mistake is, that men, finding in the rap-tures of the higher poetry a condition of exaltation, to which they have no parallel in their own experience, besides the spurious resemblance of it in dreams and fevers, impute a state of dreaminess and fever to the poet. But the true poet dreams being awake. He is not possessed by his subject, but has dominion over it.[55]

This necessary stay for mortal and mental health lies behind the fabrication in the play that Charles has engineered the *Tales from Shakespeare* to keep Mary at work, rational and so sane; but it is clearly not an attitude which Parker and Evans share. Their portraits of Coleridge and De Quincey in particular, while also factually grounded, suggest that the line between the visionary genius—often drug induced and transported from re-ality—and sanity is perilously thin and may, at times, as with Mary, cease to exist.

That Charles did not permit himself such doubts is clear from his eulogy for Coleridge written in 1834.

> When I heard of the death of Coleridge, it was without grief. It seemed to me that he long had been on the confines of the next world,—that he had a hunger for eternity. I grieved then that I could not grieve. But since, I feel how great a part he was of me. His great and dear spirit haunts me. I cannot think a thought, I cannot make a criticism on men or books, without an ineffectual turning and reference to him. He was the proof and touchstone of all my cogita-tions. . . . Great in his writings, he was greatest in his con-

versation. In him was disproved that old maxim, that we should allow every one his share of talk. He would talk from morn to dewy eve, nor cease till far midnight, yet who ever would interrupt him,—who would obstruct that continuous flow of converse, fetched from Helicon or Zion? He had the tact of making the unintelligible seem plain. . . . Never saw I his likeness, nor probably the world can see again.[56]

This was the same extravagant praise he reserved for another artist, Fanny Kelly, the actress, by 1819 "long ranked among the most considerable of our London performers." His early essay titled "Barbara S——" (her pseudonym) praises her as a child actress of eleven, but that precocity and cleverness were later to become an admirable passion for him.

> She is, in truth, no ordinary tragedian. Her Yarico is the most intense piece of acting which I ever witnessed, the most heart-rending spectacle. To see her leaning upon that wretched reed, her lover—the very exhibition of whose character would be a moral offence, but for her clinging and noble credulity—to see her lean upon that flint, and by the strong workings of passion imagine it a god—is one of the most afflicting lessons of the yearnings of the human heart and its sad mistakes, that ever was read upon a stage. The whole performance [at the Bath Theater] is every where *African*, fervid, glowing.[57]

In a letter to Wordsworth he speaks of Fanny's "divine plain face."[58] But the more tempered character of *The Coast of Illyria* is probably nearer the truth. Sir Thomas Noon Talfourd, who knew Fanny, writes in his *Memoirs of Charles Lamb* that she "became a frequent guest in Great Russell Street, and charmed the circle there by the heartiness of her manners, the delicacy and gentleness of her remarks, and her unaffected sensibility, as much as she had done on the stage."[59] Her reserve is borne out in her swift reply to Charles's proposal.

> An early & deeply rooted attachment has fixed my heart on one from whom no worldly prospect can well induce me to withdraw it but while I thus *frankly* & decidedly decline your proposal, believe me, I am not insensible to the high

honour which the preference of such a mind as yours confers upon me—let me, however, hope that all thought upon this subject will end with this letter, & that you will henceforth encourage no other sentiment towards me than esteem in my private character and a continuance of that approbation of my humble talents which you have already expressed so much & so often to my advantage and gratification.

He sent an equally swift reply: "*Your injunctions shall be obeyed to a tittle.*"[60]

But if Parker and Evans have heightened the affair between Charles and Fanny and brought it back in time in order to make Mary's role more tragic, they have not exaggerated another feature of the warm, charming, witty, affable (but stammering) Charles. It is a characteristic that must have instinctively appealed to Parker—Charles Lamb's love of puns (which occur frequently in the play). Charles remarks in "Odes and Addresses to Great People" that "A pun is good when it can rely on its single self; but, called in as an accessory, it weakens."[61] He enlarges upon his ideas in "That the Worst Puns Are the Best": "A pun is not bound by the laws which limit nicer wit. . . . The more exactly it satisfies the critical, the less hold it has upon some other faculties. The puns which are most entertaining are those which will least bear an analysis."[62] Blunden cites a pun which is also used in *The Coast of Illyria*: "'Have taken a room at 3s. a week, to be in between 5 and 8 at night, to avoid my *nocturnal* alias *knock-eternal* visitors.'"[63] Percy Fitzgerald quotes another: "'Believe me, the best acid,' he said to a friend, 'is assiduity.'"[64] But puns proved to be a mixed blessing for Charles. John Keats writes in a letter of December 1818, "I have seen Lamb lately—Brown and I were taken by Hunt to Novello's—there we were devastated and excruciated with bad and repeated puns—Brown don't want to go again."[65] What was not always appreciated in Charles, however, did allow Parker the comic relief that characterizes her other plays and at the same time permits her own special kind of wit.

But Parker and Evans employed other primary resources besides Charles Lamb's writings alone. They used Hazlitt's essay on the Lambs' Thursday nights to design the events of acts 2 and

3; they drew from P. G. Patmore's affectionate 1826 essay on Beckey—"who had honesty and wit enough to protect us from the consequences of our own carelessness or indifference"[66]—to portray the sympathetic acerbity of the housekeeper in *The Coast of Illyria*; and they transported De Quincey's moving reminiscence of the little orphan girl Ann in *Confessions of an English Opium Eater* almost verbatim into act 3. Indeed, Parker and Evans took only a few liberties. They collapsed time to intensify Mary's tragedy, coalescing the portrait of the Lamb circle around 1810 with Charles's proposal to Fanny Kelly (1819) and his retirement from East India House (1825). They also invented four characters without drawing on historical records—Mr. and Mrs. Crittenden, Mr. Wilberforce, and Mrs. Kelly; Mrs. Kelly especially resembles Mrs. Nichols in *The Ladies of the Corridor*, Mrs. Corey in *The Ice Age*, and a number of coarse, overbearing women in Parker's fiction whose character traits doubtless stem from those of her stepmother, Eleanor, and her mother-in-law, Mrs. Campbell. Emma Isola was in fact reared by Charles and Mary as their own daughter; she did not arrive walking the streets alone. And Charles, as we have seen, was not drunk when his sister murdered their mother.

The other anomaly in *The Coast of Illyria* is the Lambs' *Tales from Shakespeare*, which was published earlier than the period treated in the play (in 1807). The best description of the project is in a letter from Mary to Sarah Stoddart on June 2, 1806: "Charles has written *Macbeth*, *Othello*, *King Lear*, and has begun *Hamlet*; you would like to see us, as we often sit writing on one table (but not on one cushion sitting), like Hermia and Helena in the *Midsummer Night's Dream*; or, rather, like an old literary Darby and Joan: I taking snuff, and he groaning all the while, and saying he can make nothing of it, which he always says till he has finished, and then he finds out he has made something of it."[67] This is surely the central image behind the play, this happy vision of brother and sister, artists and geniuses in their own way, supporting, loving, and so sustaining each other through the most perilous times. It also provides the title for *The Coast of Illyria*, although the *Tales* phrases it somewhat differently: Sebastian and his sister Viola "were both born in one hour, and in one hour they were both in danger of perishing, for they were shipwrecked on the coast of Illyria as they were making a sea-voyage together."[68] Their voyage, of course, is their journey on the unpredictable sea of life, a journey which the Lambs, as they say in their Preface, wished to show was one of many in Shakespeare that serve as "enrichers of the fancy, strengtheners of virtue, a withdrawing from all selfish and mercenary thoughts, a lesson of all sweet and honourable thoughts and actions, to teach courtesy, benignity, generosity, humanity; for of examples, teaching these virtues, his pages are full."[69] But there are other prototypes of shared love of brother and sister in Shakespeare—Laertes and Ophelia, Caesar and Octavia—and in the Lambs' collection as well. Mary must have thought of Charles when writing her paraphrase of *Cymbeline*: "Imogen and Posthumus were both taught by the same masters, and were playfellows from their infancy; they loved each other tenderly when they were children, and, their affection continuing to increase with their years, when they grew up they privately married."[70] *Measure for Measure* must have been more difficult still when Claudio is made to say to Isabel, " 'The sin you do to save a brother's life, nature dispenses with the deed so far that it becomes a virtue,' " yet Isabel's thoughts about her own crime, according to Angelo, "had disordered her senses."[71] For those who attended *The Coast of Illyria* and who knew the Lambs only through the popular *Tales from Shakespeare*, the play would suggest many haunting resonances.

A review of the material on which Parker and Evans drew for *The Coast of Illyria* will account for much of the substance of the play, but it will not explain why Parker was so drawn to the Lambs or what of importance she found in their story. Yet there was much there that spoke to her basic concerns and deepest needs. For one thing, the fundamental estrangement of Mary and Charles Lamb from their invalid mother and senile father suggests the very real estrangement Dorothy Rothschild had suffered from her own parents and stepmother. In the detailed and loving relationship that develops between brother and sister in her play, she may have been compensating for her own childhood loneliness when her sister rarely spent time with her and her brothers never did;[72] more essentially, perhaps, the relationship compensates for Parker's life-long sense of guilt over the deaths of her younger sister, Eliza, and her stepmother, Eleanor. Coincidentally, Parker and Evans were relatively analogous in their ages—and in their difference in age—to Mary and Charles Lamb. What solace the Lambs worked out for each other, then, might have held some suggestions for Parker and Evans, whose relationship was much more often characterized by squabbling and by jockeying for position.

Parker also found in Charles Lamb a wit she could admire, a wit of which examples abound:

> On one occasion, an old lady was pouring into his ear a tirade, more remarkable for length than substance, when, observing that the essayist was fast lapsing into a state of oblivion, she aroused him by remarking in a loud voice, "I'm afraid, Mr. Lamb, you are deriving no benefit from my observations!" "Well, Madam!" he replied, recollecting himself, "I cannot say that I am; but perhaps the lady on the other side of me is, for they go in at one ear and out of the other."[73]

Lamb's wit promoted Thursday nights of good conversation and repartee that could serve as a nineteenth-century equivalent for—and so a measuring stick of—the Algonquin Round Table, at which Parker had established her literary encounters and reputation, and the famed salon of Neysa McMein, where Parker's wit shone daily.[74] As for the Lambs' Thursday nights, William Hazlitt reports in his essay "On the Conversation of Authors" that "Wit and good fellowship was the motto, inscribed over the door. When a stranger came in, it was not asked, 'Has he written any thing?'—we were above that pedantry; but we waited to see what he could do,"[75] just as the self-styled wits at the Algonquin Round Table and at Neysa McMein's did. "Casual, incisive, they had a terrible integrity about their work and a boundless ambition,"[76] Edna Ferber wrote about Robert Sherwood, Robert Benchley, Alexander Woollcott, Beatrice Ames, George S. Kaufmann, Marc Connelly, and others. But their gatherings were a two-edged sword. Their interest in arts and letters caused them to seek each other out—as the poets of the Romantic period did at the Lambs'—but it also caused them to compete with each other for attention and admiration—as

Coleridge and Hazlitt strive to do in *The Coast of Illyria*. Hazlitt recognizes this in an essay Parker may well have read as background to the Lambs' circle: "The art of conversation is the art of hearing as well as of being heard. Authors in general are not good listeners. Some of the best talkers are, on this account, the worst company; and some who are very indifferent, but very great talkers, are as bad. It is sometimes wonderful to see how a person, who has been entertaining or tiring a company by the hour together, drops his countenance as if he had been shot, or had been seized with a sudden lock-jaw, the moment any one interposes a single observation."[77] He also writes that the "litigious humour is bad enough: but there is one character still worse, that of a person who goes into company, not to contradict, but to *talk at* you."[78]

And with the talking, in Charles's day as in Parker's, there came the drinking; the brandy and water and the porter, which Charles supplies lavishly in *The Coast of Illyria*, had its counterparts in the parties the Algonquin wits held in Woollcott's New York apartment, in Manhattan speakeasies, at estates on Long Island, and on Neshobe Island near Bomoseen, Vermont. In *The Coast of Illyria* this gathering of self-acclaimed great writers augments alcohol with drugs. Parker and Evans are insistent that such behavior is self-destructive—for Coleridge especially, as shown throughout the play but also for De Quincey and for Charles—and the playwrights have Becky note that it can also be destructive of others, especially of Mary: "Thursday nights! All the people, all the talking, the drinking and the smoking. It was no good for poor Miss Lamb. I hope they'll stay away from now on and let her rest; her so long from home this last time." It is as if the insulated artist needs a verbal and social outlet which in turn threatens the insulation that allows his or her artistry to function, an awful paradox as true of the Algonquin circle as of the Lambs' circle; it was because of Parker's associations with writers at this time that she first began to drink excessively and first attempted suicide. She knew acts of self-destruction as Coleridge and Charles (and Mary) did. At the same time she knew, as she suggests in *The Coast of Illyria*, that such excessive behavior needs consolation and guidance, that it can be almost fatally attractive. "Preposterous. Vulnerable. Comic. Pathetic.

In short, irresistible," Mary tells Fanny. "Our great ones. You'll learn how much they are our little children." *The Coast of Illyria* means to investigate just this self-destruction coupled with irresistibility.

If Charles Lamb and his literary circle were widely known in 1948, when Parker and Evans were writing their play, Mary was even more widely known and regarded as a striking victim of gender discrimination. Anthony puts forth just such a case in her popular biography of the Lambs published in 1945.

> The bulk of the catastrophe [of aging and dependent parents] fell most unfairly, as it must have seemed to her, on her shoulders. Her brothers were slightly favoured. Through a sex discrimination she had already learned to resent, they escaped some of the misfortunes that fell to her share. Along with her parents she had dropped to a lower social level. Her brothers, having already partially climbed to a higher outlook, were able to maintain it through school associations. But Mary, as genuinely refined and cultivated as they, lapsed into sheer dull isolation, poverty, and drudgery. She became the social Ishmael she had once played at being.[79]

By 1948, Mary Lamb was generally conceded to have been a middle-aged spinster forced to remain at home to support and comfort her parents, robbed of a normal social and marital life and trapped in the confines of small family lodgings—and it was this desperate situation, moreover, that was commonly believed to have sent her mad and to have caused the killing of her mother.

Such an interpretation would have been profoundly important to Parker. "I'm a feminist," she told Marion Capron forthrightly, "and God knows I'm loyal to my sex, and you must remember that from my very early days, when this city was scarcely safe from buffaloes, I was in the struggle for equal rights for women. . . . we paraded through the catcalls of men and . . . we chained ourselves to lamp posts to try to get our equality."[80] From the beginning of her career, Parker had done the same kind of writing as the men with whom she associated, and she insisted on equal rights and comparable wages. If she did not actually join the Lucy Stone League, which demanded such treatment, she was close friends with Ruth Hale and Jane Grant, who founded it. Yet her keen awareness of discrimination must have had a close analogy in Mary Lamb's. In the days when similar Bluestocking clubs flourished in London to argue that women's minds were equal to men's, Mary could hardly have been unaware of such works as Mary Wollstonecraft's *Vindication of the Rights of Woman*, published in an early and a revised edition in 1792, four years before the murder. "Oppression thus formed many of the features of [women's] character perfectly to coincide with that of the oppressed half of mankind," Wollstonecraft had written, adding further:

> Asserting the rights which women in common with men ought to contend for, I have not attempted to extenuate their faults; but to prove them to be the natural consequence of their education and station in society. If so, it is reasonable to suppose that they will change their character, and correct their vices and follies, when they are allowed to be free in a physical, moral, and civil sense.
>
> Let women share the rights and she will emulate the virtues of man; for she must grow more perfect when emancipated, or justify the authority that chains such a weak being to her duty.—If the latter, it will be expedient to open a fresh trade with Russia for whips.[81]

Alert to her times as well as to her own confinement, Mary Lamb followed suit. Under the pseudonym "Sempronia," she published in *The British Lady's Magazine* in April 1815 her own feminist emancipation proclamation, "On Needle-work," in which her former job as mantua-maker became a badge of women's subordination and a potential source of pride when it was properly conceived and rewarded. "My strongest motive is to excite attention towards the industrious sisterhood to which I once belonged," she begins; "from books I have been informed of the fact upon which 'The British Lady's Magazine' chiefly founds its pretensions, namely, that women have of late been rapidly advancing in intellectual improvement. Much may have been gained in this way, indirectly, for that class of females for whom I wish to plead." And then comes the potent thesis: "Needle-work and intellectual improvement are naturally in a state of warfare."[82]

Since this bold statement was commonly perceived as Mary Lamb's finest hour, it is not difficult to understand why Romola Robb, when rehearsing *The Coast of Illyria* with Parker, kept having the clear sense that Parker saw herself in Mary. "On Needle-work" continues with a forceful statement that is at times assaultive and at times playful, serious and satiric by turn, as Parker often is.

Is it too bold an attempt to persuade your readers that it would prove an incalculable addition to general happiness, and the domestic comfort of both sexes, if needle-work were never practised but for a remuneration in money? As nearly, however, as this desirable thing can be effected, so much more nearly will women be upon an equality with men, as far as respects the mere enjoyment of life. As far as that goes, I believe it is every woman's opinion that the condition of men is far superior to her own.

"They can do what they like," we say. Do not these words generally mean, they have time to seek out whatever amusements suit their tastes? We dare not tell them we have no time to do this; for, if they should ask in what manner we dispose of our time, we should blush to enter upon a detail of the minutiae which compose the sum of a woman's daily employment. Nay, many a lady who allows not herself one quarter of an hour's positive leisure during her waking hours, considers her own husband as the most industrious of men, if he steadily pursue his occupation till the hour of dinner, and will be perpetually lamenting her own idleness.

Real business and *real leisure* make up the portions of men's time—two sources of happiness which we certainly partake of in a very inferior degree. To the execution of employment, in which the faculties of the body or mind are called into busy action, there must be a consoling importance attached, which feminine duties (that generic term for all our business) cannot aspire to.

In the most meritorious discharges of those duties, the

highest praise we can aim at is to be accounted the help-
mates of *man*; who, in return for all he does for us, expects,
and justly expects, us to do all in our power to soften and
sweeten life.[83]

Like Wollstonecraft, Mary Lamb calls for equal rights for education for women.

The parents of female children, who were known to be destined from their birth to maintain themselves through the
whole course of their lives with like certainty as their sons
are, would feel it a duty incumbent on themselves to
strengthen the minds, and even the bodily constitutions, of
their girls, so circumstanced, by an education which, without affronting the preconceived habits of society, might en-
able them to follow some occupation now considered above
the capacity or too robust for the constitution of our sex.
Plenty of resources would then lie open for single women to
obtain an independent livelihood, when every parent would
be upon the alert to encroach upon some employment, now
engrossed by men, for such of their daughters as would then
be exactly in the same predicament as their sons now are.[84]

Mary Lamb also promoted societal recognition of the real value
of women's work.

It would be an excellent plan, attended with very little
trouble, to calculate every evening how much money has
been saved by needle-work *done in the family*, and compare
the result with the daily portion of the yearly income. Nor
would it be amiss to make a memorandum of the time passed
in this way, adding also a guess as to what share it has taken
up in the thoughts and conversation. This would be an easy
mode of forming a true notion, and getting at the exact
worth of this species of *home* industry, and perhaps might
place it in a different light from any in which it has hitherto
been the fashion to consider it.[85]

In *The Coast of Illyria*, Parker and Evans invoke this issue of
enforced gender inferiority frequently if subtly in the treatment
of Mary and Fanny—and of Emma and Becky—by Charles and

his friends. (Next to such treatment the deference allowed George Dyer is striking.) And the issue of inferiority is also extended—properly enough—to concern for the poor and the downtrodden. Parker had been their champion all her life; she could remember, she wrote in *New Masses* in 1939, at the age of five "going to the window and seeing the street with the men shoveling snow; their hands were purple on their shovels, and their feet were wrapped with burlap. And my aunt, looking over my shoulder, said, 'Now isn't it nice there's this blizzard. All those men have work.' And I knew then that it was not nice that men could work for their lives only in desperate weather, that there was no work for them when it was fair."[86] In *The Coast of Illyria* the playwrights have Coleridge take up the cause with historical accuracy: "[W]e are in a dreadful state. One class presses with iron foot upon the wounded heads beneath. We need most deeply a reform, but not the muddling reform we shall have. The system must alter. The system must alter radically for to believe in the future one must be a radical." Coleridge is addressing the era of Napoleonic conquest; Parker is writing a play in the aftermath of the Second World War. But they share the same premise—"how different a rich country is from a happy one. Rich countries are always unhappy, miserable, degraded countries"—a premise which Mary instantly modifies: "People, too. Oh, people, too!" And by act 3 *The Coast of Illyria* is quite clear about what people Mary has in mind: Tommy Blye and Mary Blandy and the ragged crowd on the street that snatch the money Dyer meant to distribute for Charles as the mob saw fit.

The staunch and sensitive Mary Lamb of *The Coast of Illyria*—at once the cultivated hostess, the mediator in quarrels, the embodiment of kindness and generosity and wisdom, the one with clear and fixed values—is the Mary Lamb who wrote "On Needle-work"; she is also the Mary Lamb who, frustrated, confined, and depressed by her own needlework, went insane and committed murder against her chief oppressor. About this composite the play could not be more outspoken; Charles describes Mary to Fanny, most precisely, as "a medley between inspiration and possession." His remark can be interpreted to mean that she ranges between manic high spirits and gloomy depression, such as when she talks with Fanny excitedly—"We are dark and devious conspirators. We will win, my dear. Gracious, how smug you must think me with my 'we will win'! But you see, I am now decided that I shall be the only woman in the world who could welcome a brother's wife and make a friend of her"—and when she confesses to Coleridge her melancholy fears—"They tell me there's something new. It's now the fashion to have tea at Bedlam of a Sunday. They go there to laugh at the poor mad wretches chained to their beds naked. And some day they will come there and look at me! And they'll laugh at my shaved head, and they'll throw me bits of their cakes! Because that's where I'll be! That's where I'll end my days!" Mary seesaws between the peaks and valleys of her own projected self, from being a generous hostess to a public ward dependent on charity, from creating a constructive conspiracy to destroying herself (and perhaps her family too). She moves from wisdom to despair, from artistry to insanity, and back again.

This awful recognition—*her* awful recognition in the play—is the epicenter of *The Coast of Illyria*, and her mood swings and moment of truth are reflected in those of the other characters. In his famous essay "On Genius and Common Sense," Hazlitt advocates reason as "the interpreter and critic of nature and genius" although not "their lawgiver and judge,"[87] but in the play by Parker and Evans he is self-absorbed in anger and humiliation; creatively, *irrationally*, he sees himself as "the victim of the most outrageous cruelty," "a whited sepulchre containing the rotted corpse of a heart." In his *Confessions of an English Opium Eater*—what one critic has recently called "a meditation on the mechanism of the imagination"[88]—De Quincey reports that the effects of opium follow the same up-and-down radical path. On the one hand,

> . . . the primary effects of opium are always, and in the highest degree, to excite and stimulate. . . . [O]pium . . . communicates serenity and equipoise to all the faculties, active or passive: and with respect to the temper and moral feelings in general, it gives simply that sort of vital warmth which is approved by the judgment. . . . [O]pium, like wine, gives an expansion to the heart and the benevolent

affections. . . . [T]he moral affections are in a state of cloud-less serenity; and over all is the great light of the majestic intellect.[89]

But at the same time, opium-induced dreams

were accompanied by deep-seated anxiety and gloomy mel-ancholy, such as are wholly incommunicable by words. I seemed every night to descend, not metaphorically, but liter-ally to descend, into chasms and sunless abysses, depths be-low depths, from which it seemed hopeless that I could ever reascend. Nor did I, by waking, feel that I *had* reascended. This I do not dwell upon; because the state of gloom which attended these gorgeous spectacles, amounting at least to utter darkness, as of some suicidal despondency, cannot be approached by words.[90]

The effects of opium—their consequences for sanity and for art—are in fact a major concern in *The Coast of Illyria*.

Coleridge: (Re-entering with De Quincey. Coleridge has taken laudanum from De Quincey with the usual calming and lib-erating effect) And why do you seek the drug?
De Quincey: The cold and the darkness and the gray rats. . . .
Coleridge: I see. And the drug brings you riches; sleep and dreams.
De Quincey: Sometimes I lose the dreams.
Coleridge: More and more I keep them.

What follows is one of the most theatrical moments of the play, although it too is based on historic fact: Coleridge recites aloud "Kubla Khan" (which he does not name). It is his most vision-ary, creative, and drug-induced poem—as he himself says in a note published with the poem—and it too tells of the peaks and valleys of creation:

> In Xanadu did Kubla Khan
> A stately pleasure-dome decree;
> Where Alph, the sacred river, ran
> Through caverns measureless to man
> Down to a sunless sea.
>
> .   .   .   .

> But oh! that deep romantic chasm which slanted
> Down the green hill athwart a cedarn cover!
> A savage place! as old and as enchanted
> As e'er beneath a waning moon was haunted
> By woman wailing for her demon-lover!

And as confirming reprise, Coleridge's recitation concludes:

> Through wood and dale the sacred river ran,
> Then reached the caverns measureless to man,
> And sank in tumult to a lifeless ocean;
> And 'midst this tumult Kubla heard from far
> Ancestral voices prophesying war!

This recurrent alternation of moods which characterizes poets and poems in *The Coast of Illyria* precisely parallels the manic depressive nature of Mary's mental illness. One critic states that "such a disability is not usually violent, since in depression the will to act is all but paralysed, and in mania the victim exhibits a hysterical happiness in which the motivation for violence is absent. Mary's matricide came about from the combination of emotional instability with unbearable external pressures."[91] But Parker and Evans argue that just such emotional instability can be the wellspring of art. It can also lead to profound insights of a human rather than a visionary kind. When Coleridge sees genius not merely as a sickness but a curse, Mary is suddenly no longer either manic or depressive but strikingly rational.

> Oh, Coleridge, you and your shackles! You have all the freedom any man could take and it's made you its slave. What the Devil's the matter with you? What the Devil's the matter with all of you? I know I have defended your ridiculous behavior but I can find no further defense for it. You geniuses, charging about calling yourselves accursed and God Almighty; taking pride in the word. Calling yourselves lost, the whole generation of you, *lost*! Yet may God help the one who tries to rescue you. You don't want to be rescued. You want to stay lost, so you can be pitied for your weaknesses, and excused of your indulgences, and exempted from your moral taxes. Making your own rules for your own selves; too pre-

cious and free to obey the laws of human behavior. So filled
with pity for yourselves that if there is another to be pitied
you shrink away and cry, "Calamity!" Christ, if you knew
what calamity means!

It is as striking a moment as the parallel one of Coleridge's recitation, for in this play of genius shipwrecked off the coast of
Illyria who, finally, is mad and who is sane?

The answer may well be that "*there are no borderlines of insanity*";[92] such an observation is made by Dr. Eugen Bleuler in
his widely known *Textbook of Psychiatry* translated by A. A.
Brill into English in 1934. Bleuler was the distinguished psychiatrist at Burghölzli, a clinic in Europe, and was known to Parker
as the doctor who treated one of her close friends, Zelda Fitzgerald, a fellow woman writer who went mad. "There is a
connection between genius and mental abnormality," Bleuler
claims:

> The normal philistine is adjusted to the conditions in which
> he was born, and balances with their little changes without
> thinking or noticing much in the process. The psychopathic
> individual cannot adapt himself so well, or not at all; he
> reacts to difficulties resulting therefrom either by evasion,—
> he may take refuge from the demands, in hysteria or neu-
> rasthenia,—or he may create an imaginary world for himself
> through grandiose and persecutory delusion,—or aggressive-
> ly by attempts to adapt the external world to his necessities,
> or by both together. Whoever would like the outer world dif-
> ferent in large or small matters is compelled to ponder over it
> and strive for inventions, social betterments, etc. If he is also
> sufficiently intelligent, the facility of avoiding the usual
> paths may be directly conducive to finding something new.
> Often the lack of adaptability lies rather in inner difficulties,
> because the different tendencies do not equalize themselves
> but lead to a lasting inner schism. Such people may combine
> the contrasts in dereistic thinking or obtain satisfaction from
> without; if they have the other necessary qualifications,
> they become poets or artists.[93]

De Quincey's treatise on invention and Coleridge's concern for
social betterment, like Mary's imaginary worlds and Charles's

grandiose and persecutory delusions, all meet in what was called at first dementia praecox, what was thought by Zelda's time to be schizophrenia, and what by the time of *The Coast of Illyria* was being called manic depression. As Bleuler notes, the unstable mind may take refuge in alcoholism: "Drunkards are easily inclined to take up new plans, to let the old ones fall and finally not to accomplish anything worth while. The lack of a consistent mood deprives them, in the realm of character, of the *endurance* and *perseverance* of their endeavors and, in the realm of intellect, of a consistent *purpose*."[94] This is a fair characterization of Charles Lamb in *The Coast of Illyria*. Bleuler also notes that unstable minds like Mary's may take refuge in manic periods characterized by "an exalted feeling of self, euphoria, and cheerfulness" and in depressive states of anxiety when "patients like to complain that they have no emotion; everything seems colorless, and strange."[95] For such people, Bleuler says, "nothing can be done except to send them to a hospital. There the attack most easily runs its course in spite of all irritations because of the confinement. As far as possible irritants should be kept away; isolation, which still gives the patient a chance to entertain himself somehow with trifles, is the therapy which should be applied whenever possible."[96] This is the treatment Zelda Fitzgerald received first at Zurich and later at Asheville, North Carolina, in a sanitarium to which, like Mary Lamb, she would periodically commit herself when she felt herself "slipping."[97] Her behavior was reminiscent of Mary Lamb's. "When you knew Zelda as well as [Gerald and Sara Murphy] did," their friend and biographer Andrew Turnbull writes, "you discovered that in her way she was just as rare a person as Scott. She had a sweet, lasting quality that inspired affection despite her erratic, sometimes terrifying, behavior."[98] And perhaps not coincidentally, the response of her husband, Scott Fitzgerald, was to turn to alcohol, as Charles did when faced with Mary's illness. "Drink heightens feeling," Fitzgerald claimed; "When I drink, it heightens my emotions and I put it in a story."[99] He had done this when writing about himself and Zelda in *Tender Is the Night* (he even quotes directly from Bleuler's diagnosis of Zelda), and alcoholism was also the chief theme of his last works in Hollywood, the filmscript *Cosmopolitan* and the novel *The Last Tycoon*. At that time Parker had been seeing Fitzgerald again, and she was alone at his funeral in 1940, just eight years before *The Coast of Illyria*.

Other artists—other women artists especially close to Parker —suffered in similar ways. The poet Elinor Wylie had had a nervous breakdown and it was "thought she was going mad."[100] The poet Parker most emulated, Edna St. Vincent Millay, suffered from alcoholism, a nervous breakdown, and severe bouts of depression after her hospitalization in 1944, four years before *The Coast of Illyria*. Most important and most telling of all, however, Parker herself was manic depressive too and, according to her psychiatrist, Dr. Alvan Baruch, "a pathological drinker."[101] "With her classic swings of mood," her biographer writes, Parker was "a sufferer of recurrent psychosis in which periods of depression of the endogenous type were punctuated by periods of well-being and achievement, with bursts of overactivity, sometimes loquacity or euphoria (irritability, in some) amounting to mania, the swings moving from being overtly depressed to periods when she performed an above-average level of originality and productiveness."[102] She went repeatedly from graciousness, charm, hard work, and clever wit to periods of despair, exhaustion, and even attempts at suicide. "I got the impression of real pathos," Romola Robb reports. Little wonder: Parker clearly projected Mary Lamb into others she knew and saw in Mary, at least potentially, herself. By the conclusion of their play, it seems at least possible that the Illyria of Parker and Evans— like Bohemia in *The Tempest* of Shakespeare—may have no coast at all.

T*he Coast of Illyria* was apparently drafted in the spring of 1948; Margo Jones acknowledged receiving it from Parker and Evans on May 18 and promised to read it "as soon as possible."[103] But it took her nearly two months; she wrote on July 16 that an "involved trip" to Rome and London and "production problems" had intervened. "However, I have just finished reading COAST OF ILLYRIA and think it is terrific. I would like to hold on to it until I can figure what I might be able to do about it." Those she consulted apparently approved, although Jones kept no records of this; and she must have contracted the play by October 25, for she announced it as part of her Theatre '49 season. She had also hired Romola Robb for the part of Mary particularly, and she was writing Parker and Evans for pictures and biographical material for publicity. A month later, on November 14, her anticipation still ran high; she wrote Mr. and Mrs. James Moll, friends in Austin, that she was "very excited about COAST OF ILLYRIA, the play about Charles and Mary Lamb by Dorothy Parker and Ross Evans."

But by the new year, she saw that it shared with the subsequent play by Parker and d'Usseau, *The Ladies of the Corridor*, the problem of length; the first act was also patchy and confusing. Parker and Evans, meantime, proposed another change in a joint letter to Jones from their apartment in the Chateau Marmont on February 4.

> We wish so much that we could talk to you about "The Coast of Illyria." We know that it requires work, but naturally we don't want to do anything to it until we know how and what you feel about it. We have had several ideas that seemed to us important—one, in particular, that we do a very brief prologue showing the actual murder. The scene would be some ten years earlier, in a little room in the place where the Lamb family then lived. There would be in it, Mary, her mother, her father—paralyzed in his chair—and two sewing girls. The scene would be extremely brief, but we feel it would lend enormously to Mary later, when we see her sweet and strong. We would be so glad if you would think about this.

They added, "Several actresses out here seem to want to play Mary, but, of course, we have said nothing to them, because we do not know what ideas you have."

Jones sent a sobering reply by return mail on February 9.

> I was so glad to get your letter and the pictures. How I wish I could fly out and have a real talk with you! I am deeply in love with the script. My one complaint in life is time. As you know, I do a different show each three weeks. My company is small and they play eight performances a week—six nights and two matinees—so my rehearsal time is limited. I have more time this year than I did last; and I

hope next year to run the shows for four weeks so that it will give me an extra week of rehearsal. But at the present time it's almost impossible to make any changes to speak of after we go into rehearsal. Your idea about the prologue might be a wonderful one but from a casting point of view I beg you not to plan it because I am using every available Equity actor in my company and still will have to cast a couple of the small parts outside of my company. All of my actors are exceedingly good and the moment that I have to go outside of my company I feel that the quality slips. Therefore, to add any new people to the cast would be a really serious problem with me.

I have not timed the reading of your script but I feel reasonably sure that it is extremely long. My greatest aim in the theatre is to interpret what an author has written. I have never been the kind of producer or director who tries to cut scripts to pieces. I think Eddie Mayer can tell you how deeply I reverence and respect the author's words. However I am convinced that any play that runs much over two hours and ten minutes hurts itself in the long run. I would so much prefer you two to go through the script and see if you feel that there are places that you could cut it down. My bet, without timing it, is that it is thirty pages longer than the regular playing time usually is, which is approximately thirty minutes playing time. Should we plan to do the play after its production here, your idea in relation to the prologue could perhaps be added.

I do not use guest stars in my productions because we play in repertory and because I so firmly believe in ensemble work I find casting all shows within my company the best, healthiest and most exciting method. However I would be delighted to know who are some of the people you mention being interested in playing Mary because we can keep it in mind in future plans. I believe I can cast it awfully well here.

I am sure that this is going to be an exciting experience. I will keep in close touch with you. We plan to go into rehearsal March 15th. The play will open April 4th and run through April 23rd; and then, if nothing happens, we hope to repeat it during our six weeks of repertory from April 25th to June 4th.

Margo Jones was the pioneer and leader in regional repertory theater in the United States, championed by Brooks Atkinson and warmly admired throughout the country. Parker and Evans understandably listened to her and abided by her decisions. They signed a contract which jointly gave them five percent of the gross receipts, but they also asked for and received a rider which gave Jones "only the right to produce the play in Dallas" and freed the work for them to contract for production elsewhere: perhaps thoughts of New York and the Edinburgh Festival were already in the coauthors' minds.

The problem of length disappeared, at least temporarily, but the problem of casting persisted. Jones wrote Parker and Evans on February 18.

I read your play aloud the other night to my General Manager and we timed that reading, which was about two hours and ten minutes. I don't think you should do any drastic cutting. As a matter of fact, if you will still hold off on it a few more days, I will give it some real serious thought. I do have one suggestion to make in relation to a very serious casting problem I have. Would there be any way, without hurting your play, to have Charles finally read the letter from Wilberforce and not have to bring Wilberforce in? Could his happiness in seeing Fanny so outweigh his feeling for the contents of the letter that he would not be afraid to open it? The reason I suggest this is not because I do not like the scene. I do. But I honestly will have one hell of a time casting the character of Wilberforce. Within my company I have a really excellent person for every single other part. But the one really old character man I have will have to play George Dyer. The next two mature men I have, who are both excellent actors, will need to play Lamb and Coleridge. The next two, who are a bit younger, will need to play Hazlitt and De Quincey and I have a boy who can play Mr. Crittenden. But these are all the men I have in my company and it's nigh unto impossible to find a good character man here who can give the rehearsal time that my regular company gives. Does this idea strike you as plausible?

She also asked them to delay their visit to Dallas, during which they planned to attend rehearsals and to rewrite the play as necessary.

During the first two weeks when the kids are trying to learn their lines and I am trying to pound characterization and business into their heads in the short hours that we have, I feel that you will be going through hell wanting to work and think on the subtler things that can easily be done in the early stages of rehearsal when a company is spending their entire time on one script. To accomplish what we have to accomplish in the first two weeks, I really have to be a slave driver to be able to get the show in shape to be worked on. I think, psychologically, that if you could arrive the Sunday a week before our opening we could have the play in good enough shape that the company would feel more relaxed in relation to our all working together. I think I know just how you both must feel about wanting to be here every minute from the beginning and I can assure you that you will be welcome and any decision you make about it will be fine. My own advice on the matter, as the result of my experience here, would be that we can get more done with the least wear and tear if you can be with me the week before and a week or two afterwards. Feel perfectly free to be very honest about your reactions to this. I will certainly understand . . .

She closed by saying, "I fall more and more in love with your script every day."

Parker and Evans agreed to Jones's suggestions. On March 18 they sent her "insert pages" that provided "as painless an elimination of Mr. Wilberforce as possible." They also delayed their trip, wiring Jones on March 25 at the Stoneleigh Hotel, where she maintained her Dallas home, "ARRIVING DALLAS 630 PM SUNDAY FLIGHT 100 AMERICAN AIRLINES PLEASE DO NOT MEET US AT THE AIRPORT FOR WE WILL PROBABLY HUG YOU TO DEATH LOVE DOROTHY AND ROSS."

They duly arrived March 27, and Jones wrote about them in her weekly Wednesday letter to her family in Livingston, Texas, on March 30.

> Dear Mother, Dad and Charles:
> . . . I will just have to admit that I am the busiest I have ever been before, but we will get the last show on next Monday and from then on out it should not be nearly so difficult this year. The authors of the play arrived last Sunday and we have had a double responsibility of taking care of them, having them at rehearsals, etc. The play is a terribly interesting one but much too long and has required a lot of cutting and re-writing, which is extremely tedious at this stage of the game. They are both very sweet people and are easy to work with. They are not accustomed to the pace that I have to keep, so I find myself having to keep them organized all the time to get the work done. I am grateful that they are such simple nice people and I think they are grateful to find us like we are.

She wrote them again, unexpectedly, on April 2, two days before the opening.

> Well, this has really been a week. I honestly do not ever remember of [sic] working harder. But everybody involved in our present production, including our two guest authors, has been sweet, kind and helpful. The problems were reasonably serious as the new script in its first form was almost an hour too long. Well, I am glad to report that with a tremendous amount of work, an hour has been cut out of the script and it actually is much better now because the extraneous material is gone and the true, moving, dramatic material remains. It has been hard, though, because it is very tedious work after actors have learned lines to either cut them out or change them. There is still a lot of work that we would like to do but we are so aware of our limited time before opening that we are trying to hold back and get what we have in smooth shape and then after we open we will still have time to improve the script. Our authors plan to remain a week after we open.

Parker sat, candid and alert, through the last week of rehearsals, one crew member recalls, wearing pants and loafers; she was accompanied by Evans and usually sipped a cup of coffee.[104] There must have been major changes, for the script extant is one-third longer and the order of characters does not agree with the cast listing in the program. But though Parker was protective of Evans, Jed Mace remembers,[105] to both cast and public she was, according to the April 18 issue of *Time* magazine, sweet and even shy. The playwrights stayed near Jones at the Stoneleigh Hotel.

Theatre '49—it was renumbered each season—had recently staged world premieres of Tennessee Williams's *Summer and Smoke* and *Leaf and Bough*, both of which went on to Broadway, and there were similar hopes for *The Coast of Illyria*. The theater itself was the former Gulf Oil Playhouse in the Texas State Fair building in Dallas, which was unusual in its arena staging and intimate in its size (Jennifer Jones's father, who owned a chain of movie theaters, had donated 199 seats because 200 or more meant that Equity payments tripled). Because it was an easy set to research, Mace built everything in his own storerooms and provided understated antiques and only books published during or before the Lambs' lifetimes. But he made the room that of a manor house rather than a town house, and he eliminated the Hogarth and the laudanum pipe.

On April 13, Jones wrote about the opening to Jonas Silverstone in New York City.

> We have been knocking ourselves out on our final production, THE COAST OF ILLYRIA which, I am glad to report, is a roaring success. Local reviews were excellent and, as you know, Mr. Atkinson's review was negative but I was very happy about his visit and all the nice things he said about our setup. We are doing the biggest business of the season and of course it's very gratifying. I was crazy about the authors, both Dorothy Parker and Ross Evans, and found them wonderful to work with.

She added in her letter a schedule for her end-of-season festival, which brought *The Coast of Illyria* back for matinee and evening performances on two Saturdays, May 28 and June 4. As she noted, the Dallas papers were kind. John Rosenfield, a staunch supporter of Jones and her theater, wrote the following review published in the *Dallas News* on April 5.

The brand new Dorothy Parker–Ross Evans play, "The Coast of Illyria" had a triumphant beginning Monday at the hands of Theater '49. First nighters found it so filled with literary substance and good theater that it is hardly possible that its history will end where it started, on the Gulf Playhouse's tiny arena stage.

The literary substance is not so much the characters, the Lambs and their Thursday night circle, as the craft with which the authors have incorporated the documented mots of the period into the text. Then they have added wit and wisdom of their own, worthy commodities from esteemed sources.

The first of the three acts, showing paste and patches, played well enough. The other two broke loose from the play-doctoring labors of authors and director and garnered responses, both jocund and tragic, for all intended points.

Audience acceptance had reached belligerent enthusiasm by the second intermission. The final walk-around by the actors was an ovation and the cries for authors were universal and genuine. A shaky Miss Parker and a pale Mr. Evans arose from sheltered corner seats in Section B. . . .

The first night was remarkably glib and well-managed. The play needs, however, considerable application of nuance, which probably was beyond the range of the rehearsal period. The jug-heads and dope-fiends, it must be said, behaved in the raw and simple style of "Ten Nights in a Bar Room." It was difficult to tell them drunk from sober. And stimulants, we have heard, bring a certain repose, hence their popularity. . . .

Romola Robb captured all acting honors as Mary and, indeed, suggested the archness that her colleagues must play up to. She masked her youthful good looks with chalky make-up and house bonnet, was always the woman of sorrow and blood-guilt. With measured virtuosity, she erupted into the mad creature bound for the snake pit of Bedlam.

Those of us who have admired Miss Robb's range and technical assurance were gratified at her ability to command the stage when necessary and to assert power, both quiet and frenzied.

The same day, Tuesday, April 5, Clay Bailey reported on the play in the *Dallas Daily Times Herald*.

Closely related to a historical situation concerning two picturesque literary figures, the Parker-Evans opus may or may not limn correctly the personalities of these figures.

What there is no uncertainty about is this—"The Coast of Illyria" is a terrific play, which supplies a mounting series of excitements, dramatic as well as comical. Its lines establish a new literary high for Theatre '49 "firsts" and the movement of the opus is spirited, logical, and completely convincing. . . .

Attending the opening was a capacity audience, with enthusiasm for the play running high and predictions for a Broadway future freely predicted. Also present were Miss Parker and Mr Evans.

There were also reviews from New York. On April 13, *Variety* noted that the play was "written with intelligence and taste, the lines . . . sharp-edged and convincing. . . . 'Illyria' is by far the best original script presented by Theatre '49 to date and is drawing capacity crowds each performance." Stringing for the *New York Times*, Rosenfield was more subdued in a review published on the morning of April 6.

The wit as well as the narrative facts are reasonably well documented as students of the period know. The authors took romantic liberties with the Charles Lamb–Fanny Kelly amour, but in a nice way that won't scare off the movies.

With authors and director still laboring over the script, the first act moved hectically and in too many directions. The other two were compact and powerful and pointed steadily to the denouement. Charles and Mary Lamb, brother and sister, needed each other too desperately to separate.

"The Coast of Illyria" was well cast within the limitations of a resident company, with Romola Robb winning the warmest appreciation for her portrayal of the occasionally mad but usually serene and patient Mary Lamb.

Rosenfield added a final caveat: "The appeal of both characters and dialogue is fundamentally literary and could be lost on a heterogeneous audience."

Jones was right in giving some emphasis to Atkinson's review, for it probably precluded, in time, a Broadway production. It appeared in a larger and more positive story on Theatre '49 and on Jones herself published in the *New York Times* on April 13.

As its final production for the season, Theatre '49 is pre-senting a play about Charles and Mary Lamb by Dorothy Parker and Ross Evans. "The Coast of Illyria" they call it, in memory of the mythical shore where Shakespeare once ship-wrecked a brother and sister. Fortunately, Dallas playgoers like the Lamb drama very much, laughing at the grumbling humors and enjoying the egotistical melancholy of Cole-ridge, Hazlitt, De Quincey, Fanny Kelly and George Dyer.

But for the record, this rapidly decentralizing critic is bound to report that in his opinion "The Coast of Illyria" is a surprisingly conventional drama, written without distinc-tion and too willing to be fascinated by the company of some early nineteenth century Grub Street scribblers.

To give their drama form Miss Parker and Mr. Evans have been obliged to impart to Lamb's genial and pedestrian chro-nology more speed and decision than it had, which is no mortal iniquity. But they have also represented him as being a passionate, desperately romantic and heartbroken suitor to Miss Kelly. This is a more independent contribution to his-tory and should be tentatively referred to the raised-eyebrows department for further study and counsel.

The most disappointing aspect of "The Coast of Illyria" is the fact that it is an ordinary drama about some extraordi-nary people. It does not penetrate very deeply into the pri-vate agony of a brother and sister condemned to a circumscribed life by her tragic insanity. As a matter of fact, Lamb and his sister are interesting rather than dramatic people and perhaps the amiable Bohemianism of "The Coast of Illyria" represents the extent of their contribution to human experience. The drama is not very vigorous or searching enough for more than an evening of ordinary theatre.

Margo Jones, the supernatural chatelaine of Theatre '49, has directed the performance with her familiar thoroughness and animation. Apart from three neatly sketched, sardonic characterizations of De Quincey by John Hudson, Coleridge by Edwin Whitner and Hazlitt by Clinton Anderson, the performance is pretty much on a level with the script. The acting is competent but not distinguished.

Clay Bailey paraphrased many of these comments in his second review of the play, published in the *Dallas Daily Times Herald* on April 13. Jones herself may have partly agreed with it, for on May 7 she wrote to Atkinson, ". . . I want to thank you for the wonderful article you did as the result of your visit here. I agree with you that there was much lacking in the ILLYRIA production and script and your comments were terrifically constructive to me." Parker and Ross returned to Hollywood four days after the show opened; on June 6, Tad Adoue III, the company manager, sent them their final royalty check.

Almost two decades later, and with justification given its styles, Parker told Richard Lamparski in a radio show that the play "was just plain silly. It was so full of atmosphere that there was nothing else in it. It was about Charles and Mary Lamb and their circle and then nothing happened at all, nothing whatever."[106] But she was sixty by then and disparaging nearly everything—the Algonquin wits, all of her poetry (which she thought imitative of Millay), and even her inability to write. In the instance of *The Coast of Illyria*, however, it was a cynicism born of bitterness, for Parker and Evans had worked hard at revising the play and for some time attempted to arrange subsequent productions. In their efforts they were sustained by Margo Jones. As soon as Atkinson's review appeared, on April 13, she wrote to the two of them, who had by now returned to Hollywood, "Illyria doing best business any production ever done here. Atkinson's article not good. Please don't worry. Play gets better every day. Cannot wait for your return." On June 6 she was pleased to report in a swift night wire that "Illyria closed season beautifully and successfully" and

added, "Letter on way." The letter was full of earnest and urgent encouragement.

> Now I want to know what you two cuties are planning to
> do about this play. This is a *very* good play. It has been
> proven. The audience consistently filled every seat and loved
> it. I personally think it needs about two more weeks work—
> which, if we had the time together, could be done. Now I
> don't want you to let life in Hollywood get in the way of
> carrying this script on to its destination. Do you have any
> plans about being East this summer? I will be in New York
> from the last week in June on until September. If I had the
> money, I would come on out to Hollywood now and stick
> right with you. If there is a possibility of our getting together
> this summer, I will try to see what I can do about writing
> down everything that I think about this script. It has gotten
> completely in my blood and I think it's an excellent script
> and no reason in the world why it should not be enormously
> successful in New York. You did a magnificent job on it here.
> How you did it, I will never know but, believe me, if we
> could work the same amount of time that we did here, to-
> gether again, I believe you would have as sound a script as is
> possible.

Parker and Evans invited Jones to Hollywood. The next record
is her letter to them on her return to Dallas on June 30.

> We have a beautiful, beautiful play. I am so happy about it
> that I could sing. It was Heaven working with you
> again. . . . Don't let this movie script annoy you. Anything
> you touch will be better—and let that give you satisfaction.
> As soon as you get it conquered—which I know you will in
> two minutes—jump onto Fanny. I shall be looking forward
> with real joy to our script. It goes round and round in my
> mind, bringing nothing but pleasure.

But she heard nothing from them: perhaps they were caught up
in their script for Bogart; perhaps they were distracted because
at one point Parker was ill with a bad liver and had to be hospi-
talized for tests; perhaps they had spent energy working on the
possibilities for the 1949 Edinburgh Festival, for which the play
had already been booked for them by Henry Sherek, Ltd., for

sixty percent of the net proceeds. Surely they were indecisive. The minutes of the Programme Committee for the Edinburgh Festival Society, Ltd., note that on February 8, 1949, Parker changed the Edinburgh title from *The Incomparable Sister* to *The Coast of Illyria*, as it was to play in Dallas; a later entry on March 29 notes that Parker had revised the script (perhaps the revisions she and Evans made in Dallas with Jones) and had still another title—this time *Mary is from Home*—but the committee denied this change because their brochure was already in print and they were fearful of public confusion and the difficulty of box office administration. Still later, on June 21, the committee's minutes record that Flora Robeson, who was to play Mary Lamb, "has now declined to perform this revised version. No compromise had been possible, and Mr. Henry Sherek had intimated that he was unable to present 'Mary is from Home'"; the Festival substituted a new play, *The Man in the Raincoat*, by Peter Ustinov.

Sherek seems not to have shared the news about the play's being dropped with Parker and Evans, however, until August 1, when word came to them through her agent Harold Freedman.

> I have just had a very depressing letter from Sherek reading as follows.
> "I have not been able to do the Parker play at Edinburgh because, confidentially, it has been turned down by every first class Director here. I tried to get Murray Macdonald, Norman Marshall and Michael Benthall, amongst others, but they all hated it and unless I can get a play directed by a first class man I cannot put it on, so you must now tell me what I am to do. Anyway, I know you would never have passed a second-class Director nor would a second-class Director have got any actor or actress, of the class to which I am now accustomed, to work under his direction."
> As you know, Ross advised me not to press Sherek for the signed contract which gives him the right to produce in London as well as Edinburgh as he thought you wanted to wait to see how matters developed with Margo Jones.
> I can, of course, write Sherek and tell him what I think of his behavior under the circumstances, which unfortunately will not do much good, but I can insist with him that he

owes us the advance on the basis of the contract which gives
him until February to produce and ask him to try to get
some one else. My own feeling, however, inasmuch as the
whole thing was based on Robeson and apparently they have
been able to find an out for Robeson on the basis of his being
unable to get a good director, so that Sherek is probably
looking for the best "out" he can get. As I told you, I have
always been afraid that we were taking chances with his
ability to put things through and if he were not able to put
them through for one reason or another he would not take
the responsibility.

I am desperately sorry about this but it may be by this
time that you have already gone ahead with your work with
Miss Jones and that an American production will still even-
tuate. In any case let me know what you want to do.

Appeals from Jones to Parker and Evans on July 20 and August
8 asking them how they were progressing with revisions went
unheeded until August 12, when they wrote her, "We've finished
the first act revision. We enclose a letter from Harold Freedman
concerning Sherek which in itself is no excuse for a slow-down,
but it may have contributed," and then added almost curtly,
"Oh. We read your suggestion of Jane Cowl for Mary Lamb.
Margo, it must be awfully hot in New York." Ten days later, on
August 22, Jones replied, "For the records, I don't believe a word
of the letter from Mr. Sherek. He evidently wanted some excuse
but he is not very imaginative," and wrote, "Now . . . you just
go on and finish up those last two acts and send the script on to
me and let's figure then what the next step is." This time there
was never a response.

Jones's extraordinarily well-preserved papers suggest that she
never heard from Parker again. But she did, in time, hear from
Evans. The two had left Hollywood by January 1950 for a vacation in Mexico, but they fought and Evans sent her off—she
flew directly to New York City—while he remained in Mexico.
On January 27, 1951, nearly a year later, he wrote to Jones from
Cuernavaca.

About one hundred years ago I was born in New York, the
most homeless hometown yet devised, so it is small wonder
that when I pulled a tired and dusty De Soto into Cuer-

navaca last March I awakened my Boxer and confided in him:

"We're here at last, Buster. Home."

And I have felt that way ever since. I've driven about ten thousand miles over this strange land but I never fail to have that "being back" feeling when I come into the little square in Cuernavaca. After sitting in Hollywood for two years this little country town had some of the appeal of Shangri-Lah [sic], but without the picturesqueness. Life after all, and despite some of my earlier convictions, can be still lived gracefully, and quietly, and without fear of neuroses. This, I suppose, might be justly called a parable. A parable of the Man Who Looked A Little Beyond His Nose.

I digress.

To keep my small house operating with a reasonable degree of comfort, to buy music and books, in short, to support myself I write stories, very slowly I write them. All I have found necessary is that one of five be accepted by a magazine. Hence I go on.

Earlier in the same letter he had written,

When is your Festival this year, Margo? I am coming up to the border sometime in March (and not coming up for air particularly) and Dallas isn't too forbidding a trip for me; particularly in ratio to my craven desire to see a play again. I've been here a year and the only thing I can faintly describe as "live entertainment" that has passed before these ever weakening eyes is a cruelly exhausted circus, one interminable feature-length movie with Cantinflas finally yielding everything to play the tragedian, and one travelling tent show which reminded me, in a curious inversion of theatrical history, of a road company Commedia d'elle Arte. In short I would be enormously pleased to once again hear a speech spoken trippingly. Send me one of those shiny little programs of yours, please.

The letter concluded, "About Dorothy I have so little news. She left Mexico after we had been here a month. This so-called Land of Enchantment hardly amused Milady. She, as you probably know, remarried her husband (a resumption of a time-tested habit and I think a good one for her) and as far as I know she is once again in the land of milk and soundtracks." Jones sent him the schedule he requested and urged him to write a new play for her. On May 30, he reported glumly that his papers had expired and that he was unable to come to Dallas. But "Bless you, dear Margo, and bless all your works. I want your season to be a record breaker in every way. . . . I want very much to see you in the Fall. I want particularly to see you with your shoes off with a battered copy of a script of mine in the seat next you." She wrote him in turn on June 29: "I am so glad that you are working on a play. How close is it to completion? If completed, will you mail it to me immediately. I may have told you this before—two of the scripts we did in Dallas last year will be done in New York this season." But she did not hear from him again.

Margo Jones did not forget *The Coast of Illyria*, however. In 1952 she sent to the William Morris Agency in New York the synopses of thirteen plays for a literary series on television. The Parker-Evans play was one of them. Some the agency thought acceptable; others it did not. Of *The Coast of Illyria* the agency representative wrote, "This cheerful little piece is completely unacceptable. This might have come in like a lamb, but came out a lion." This is the same sort of bad pun that Charles Lamb, and perhaps Parker, would have liked; but unlike Jones, the writer misreads both the intention and the accomplishment of the work. Nowhere else would Dorothy Parker ever wrestle with herself in quite this way; nowhere else would she persistently probe the issues of genius and madness, of alcoholism and drugs and art, of women's rights and the plight of the poor, and the cost and anxiety, sweetness and anguish of one person's love for another. "When I worked with Parker," Romola Robb remembers, "I kept thinking she saw herself in Mary Lamb." She probably did: the Mary Lamb of *The Coast of Illyria* is her finest tribute as it was her finest hour.

A Note on the Text

The text of *The Coast of Illyria* that is reproduced here for the first time is from the sole extant typescript, with some corrections in hand by Parker. It is one-third longer than the acted version and retains the original opening (unlike that used for performance, according to the cast listing in the program) and includes the original portrait of Mr. Wilberforce. A few obvious errors have been silently emended and certain incidentals made consistent.

Notes

1. Interview with Romola Robb Allrud, New York City, April 25, 1987.

2. Marion Meade, *Dorothy Parker: What Fresh Hell Is This?* (New York, 1988), 334.

3. Anne Gilchrist, *Mary Lamb* (Boston, 1883), 1.

4. Margo Jones, *Theatre-in-the-Round* (New York, 1951), 172–73.

5. Katharine Anthony, *The Lambs: A Story of Pre-Victorian England* (New York, 1945), 62–63.

6. Anthony, 99–100.

7. Quoted in Edmund Blunden, comp. *Charles Lamb: His Life Recorded by his Contemporaries* (London, 1934), 30–31.

8. Thomas De Quincey, *The English Mail Coach and Other Writings* (Edinburgh, 1862), 38.

9. Night Letter, box 25, folder 1, Margo Jones Collection, Texas/Dallas History and Archives Collection, Dallas Public Library.

10. Interview with Romola Robb Allrud, April 25, 1987.

11. E. V. Lucas, ed., *The Letters of Charles Lamb to which are added those of his sister Mary Lamb* (London, 1935), 1: 39–41.

12. *Letters* 1: 42–43.

13. Neil Bell (Stephen Southwold), *So Perish the Roses* (New York, 1940), 187–90.

14. Bell, 228.

15. Interview with Arnaud d'Usseau, New York City, June 15, 1987; according to d'Usseau, Parker's favorite playwrights were Ibsen, Shaw, and Chekhov.

16. Marion Capron, "Dorothy Parker," in *Writers at Work*, ed. Malcolm Cowley (New York, 1959), 79.

17. Meade, 124.

18. Robert Benchley, *Life* (December 18, 1924), 18. Cf. Heywood Broun, "Seeing Things at Night," *World* (December 1, 1924); Alexander Woollcott, *Sun* (December 1, 1924); John Anderson, *Post* (December 1,

1924); Robert Littell, "Main Street in the Theatre," *New Republic* (December 24, 1924), 20.

19. Heywood Broun, *World* (December 7, 1924), Metropolitan section.

20. *Close Harmony; or, The Lady Next Door* (New York [1929]), 85.

21. *Close Harmony*, 91.

22. Quoted in John Keats, *You Might As Well Live: The Life and Times of Dorothy Parker* (New York, 1970), 102; Richard Lamparski, "High Tea with Dorothy Parker," an unedited taped interview for WBAI, New York, lent to me by George Baxt.

23. "High Tea with Dorothy Parker."

24. Willa Cather, *A Lost Lady* (New York, 1923; 1972 Vintage ed.), 110.

25. *A Lost Lady*, 139–40.

26. *A Lost Lady*, 24.

27. *A Lost Lady*, 153, 155.

28. *The Ladies of the Corridor* (New York, 1954), 97.

29. *The Ladies of the Corridor*, 112.

30. *The Ladies of the Corridor*, 58.

31. Eric Bentley, *The Dramatic Moment* (New York, 1954), 154.

32. *New York Times* 3 (October 18, 1953): 4–5.

33. Interview with d'Usseau, June 15, 1987.

34. *The Ladies of the Corridor*, 42.

35. *The Ladies of the Corridor*, 45.

36. *The Ladies of the Corridor*, 49.

37. *The Ladies of the Corridor*, 113.

38. *The Ladies of the Corridor*, 28–29.

39. *The Ladies of the Corridor*, 86.

40. *The Ladies of the Corridor*, 108.

41. "High Tea with Dorothy Parker."

42. Interview with d'Usseau, June 15, 1987.

43. Act 2, scene 1, p. 9. The only copy of *The Ice Age* is a typescript held in the Rare Books and Manuscripts Division of the Columbia University Library.

44. Act 2, scene 1, p. 5.

45. Meade, 330.

46. J. Bryan III, *Merry Gentlemen (and One Lady)* (New York, 1986), 117.

47. Quoted in Ernest C. Ross, *The Ordeal of Bridget Elia* (Norman, Okla., 1940), 180–81.

48. Ross, 34.

49. Charles Lamb to Dorothy Wordsworth, June 14, 1805, in *Letters* 1: 394–95.

50. E. V. Lucas, ed., *The Works of Charles and Mary Lamb* (London, 1903), 4: 22–23.

51. *Works* 1: 134, 135, 139; the text is that of 1822.

52. *Works* 2: 75, 76.

53. *Works* 2: 195.

54. *Works* 1: 71–72, 76. The poetic lines are inscribed by Hogarth under the plate.

55. *Works* 2: 187.

56. *Works* 1: 351–52.

57. *Works* 1: 185–86.

58. Cited by E. V. Lucas in *The Life of Charles Lamb* (New York, 1905), 2: 19.

59. Thomas Noon Talfourd, *Memoirs of Charles Lamb*, edited and annotated by Percy Fitzgerald (London, 1892), 84.

60. Quoted in Lucas, *Life* 2: 23.

61. *Works* 4: 286.

62. *Works* 2: 257–58.

63. Edmund Blunden, *Charles Lamb and His Contemporaries* (Cambridge, England, 1933), 82.

64. Percy Fitzgerald, *Charles Lamb: His Friends, His Haunts, and His Books* (London, 1866), 157.

65. *Charles Lamb: His Life Recorded by his Contemporaries*, 91.

66. *Charles Lamb: His Life Recorded by his Contemporaries*, 161.

67. *Charles Lamb: His Life Recorded by his Contemporaries*, 42.

68. Charles and Mary Lamb, *Tales from Shakespeare* (London, 1962 ed.), 168.

69. *Tales*, 8.

70. *Tales*, 88.

71. *Tales*, 160, 163.

72. See Leslie Frewin, *The Late Mrs. Dorothy Parker* (New York, 1986), chaps. 1–3.

73. William Harness, "Lamb," in *Personal Reminiscences*, ed. Richard Henry Stoddard (New York, 1875), 238.

74. Meade, 80–81; Brian Gallagher, *Anything Goes: The Jazz Age Adventures of Neysa McMein and Her Extravagant Circle of Friends* (New York, 1987), chap. 5.

75. *Collected Works of William Hazlitt*, ed. A. R. Waller and Arnold Glover (London, 1903), 7: 36–37.

76. Quoted in Frewin, 45.

77. Hazlitt, *Works* 7: 39.

78. Hazlitt, *Works* 7: 34.

79. Anthony, 28–29.

80. Capron, 77.

81. Mary Wollstonecraft, *Vindication of the Rights of Woman*, ed. Charles W. Hagdeman, Jr. (New York, 1967), 286–87.

82. *Works* 1: 176.

83. *Works* 1: 177.

84. *Works* 1: 178–79.

85. *Works* 1: 180.

86. "Not Enough," *New Masses* (March 14, 1939), 3.

87. Hazlitt, *Works* 6: 31.

88. Alethea Hayter, "Introduction" to *Confessions of an English Opium Eater* (Harmondsworth, England, 1971), 7.

89. *Confessions*, 77, 74, 75.

90. *Confessions*, 103.

91. Winifred F. Courtney, *Young Charles Lamb 1775–1802* (New York, 1982), 236.

92. Professor Dr. Eugen Bleuler, *Textbook of Psychiatry*, trans. A. A. Brill (New York, 1934), 170.

93. Bleuler, 172.

94. Bleuler, 309.

95. Bleuler, 466, 472.

96. Bleuler, 491.

97. Andrew Turnbull, *Scott Fitzgerald* (New York, 1962), 323.

98. Turnbull, 166.

99. Turnbull, 259.

100. Stanley Olson, *Elinor Wylie: A Life Apart* (New York, 1979), 311.

101. Frewin, 105.

102. Frewin, 168.

103. The Margo Jones Collection is held in the Texas/Dallas History and Archives Collection of the Dallas Public Library. The letters and reviews referred to in the following pages can be found in box 4, folder 7; box 23, folder 24; box 25, folder 1; box 32, folders 13 and 17; box 42, folder 5; and box 93, folder 45.

104. Interview with Jed Mace, Dallas, April 4, 1987.

105. Interview with Mace, April 4, 1987.

106. "High Tea with Dorothy Parker." By current standards, the attempted period language by which *The Coast of Illyria* is meant to meld with actual quotations from the writings of the Lambs, Coleridge, Hazlitt, and De Quincey, combined with twentieth-century slang and clear Parkerisms, can seem to want discipline. Clearly, for Parker, it was the substance that counted.

Left to right: Ross Evans, Flic, and Dorothy Parker. An advance
publicity still taken at their home, Château Marmont, on Sunset
Boulevard in Hollywood.

Back row, left to right: Edwin Whitner (Coleridge), Clinton Anderson
(William Hazlitt), Harold Webster (George Dyer), and Wilson Brooks
(Charles Lamb). Front row, left to right: John Hudson (Thomas
De Quincey), Dorothy Parker, Ross Evans, and Romola Robb (Mary
Lamb).

The set for The Coast of Illyria, *by Jed Mace, the company's production designer. Mace used authentic period books and furniture, but his open set eliminated the fireplace as well as walls for hanging the Hogarth prints. The scene is the sitting room of Charles and Mary Lamb's residence in London.*

Left to right: Wilson Brooks (Charles Lamb), Edwin Whitner (Coleridge), and Romola Robb (Mary Lamb).

Left to right: Harold Webster (George Dyer), Frances Waller (Fanny Kelly), Wilson Brooks (Charles Lamb), and Romola Robb (Mary Lamb).

Left to right: Romola Robb (Mary Lamb), Wilson Brooks (Charles Lamb), and Frances Waller (Fanny Kelly).

Left to right: Wilson Brooks (Charles Lamb), Romola Robb (Mary Lamb), Edwin Whitner (Coleridge), and Frances Waller (Fanny Kelly).

Left to right: Edwin Whitner (Coleridge), Rebecca Hargis (Emma Isola), Wilson Brooks (Charles Lamb), Margaret McDonald (Becky), and Romola Robb (Mary Lamb).

Back row, left to right: Clinton Anderson (William Hazlitt) and Harold Webster (George Dyer). Middle row, left to right: Edwin Whitner (Coleridge), Romola Robb (Mary Lamb), and Wilson Brooks (Charles Lamb). Seated: John Hudson (Thomas De Quincey).

In performance, left to right: Edwin Whitner (Coleridge), Wilson Brooks (Charles Lamb), and Romola Robb (Mary Lamb).

The Coast of Illyria

A PLAY IN THREE ACTS

BY DOROTHY PARKER AND

ROSS EVANS

"There were a brother and sister . . .

who were shipwrecked off the coast of Illyria."

—*Lambs'* Tales: Twelfth Night

THE CHARACTERS

(In order of appearance)

FANNY KELLY	MRS. KELLY
CHARLES LAMB	WILLIAM HAZLITT
GEORGE DYER	THOMAS DE QUINCEY
BECKY	MR. WILBERFORCE
EMMA ISOLA	MRS. CRITTENDEN
COLERIDGE	MR. CRITTENDEN
MARY LAMB	

SYNOPSIS OF SCENES

The scene is Charles and Mary Lamb's room in London.

The time is the early nineteenth century.

ACT ONE

Scene 1. An afternoon in early autumn
Scene 2. A few hours later

ACT TWO

A Thursday evening, a month later

ACT THREE

A Thursday evening, a week later

ACT ONE : SCENE 1

Time: Late afternoon.

Scene: The flat is a spacious, well-worn home, but obviously
   not the home of wealthy people. There is a meagerness
   about the furnishings: good taste spread thin.

   In the corner, stage right, is a liquor cabinet with a few
empty bottles on its shelves. Continuing to the left, we see a
door which suggests an inner room. There is a large fireplace
centrally located. Further left a cabinet stands in the corner.
It is filled with glasses, mugs, etc. In the panel between the
door and the fireplace we see waist-high book-shelves
crowded with books, well-used books. Above the book-
shelves hang two Hogarth prints. Above the mantelpiece
hangs a large painting of a kneeling girl. In her right arm she
holds a lamb while her left arm holds a spray of roses. The
figure has a limpid beauty. At each corner of the mantelpiece, a figurine, one a shepherd, one a shepherdess. In the
panel between the fireplace and the left corner of the room
we see more book-shelves, similar in structure and contents
to the others. Above these shelves hangs one more Hogarth
print. Downstage right is a buffet table, lighted by candles
and partially set with bowls, plates, glasses, etc. Balancing
this table on the left is another table about the same size. At
present it is covered with a large cloth which conceals manuscript paper, ink wells, quills, etc. There are two chairs arranged around the fireplace; two more chairs are behind the
buffet table; one chair is upstage and centered. There is a
central entranceway, arched. Straight through the archway
is the door to the dining room. To the right is the scullery.
Downstage right is another door leading to the inner room.
The last entrance is stage left, opposite the door to the inner
room. This is the entrance from the street.

   As the curtain goes up we see Charles Lamb and Fanny
Kelly onstage alone. Charles is a slender man in his middle
thirties. Fanny is in the radiance of her early twenties. She
has a beautiful figure and she is elegantly dressed in street
costume. Charles is coatless. Fanny has great poise and style.
Charles has great sensitivity and kindness and warmth. Now

Fanny is vainly trying to free her hands from Charles'. There is a gay intimacy between them.

Fanny: Kindly let me go, Mr. Lamb.
Charles: You ask the impossible, Miss Kelly.
    (He kisses her)
    Please don't go.
Fanny: I must, Charles. I'm late for rehearsals now.
Charles: Be ten minutes later. Ah, Fanny, we have so little time together.
Fanny: And we always spend it so wisely. Wailing about how little it is. I'll be back soon.
Charles: It'll be a hundred years.
Fanny: Two hundred for me. By the time you've brought your sister home, I'll be back. I'll come straight here from the Drury Lane.
Charles: When it takes you away from me, it's the Dreary Lane. It's a pun, Fanny, it's a pun.
Fanny: I even love your puns. God's sakes, I'm in a desperate condition.
    (Fondly)
    You make the worst puns in all the world.
Charles: The worse they are the better they are. That's the law.
Fanny: That's what I said—your puns are the best in the world. Please, please, Charles. I must go.
Charles: The one afternoon I escape the office early. The one time I escape from my cage, and you must go to rehearsals! Oh! And I went through the lowest depth of hell placating Mr. Wilberforce to gain my freedom.
Fanny: Are people called Wilberforce? Who is Mr. Wilberforce?
Charles: (Mock reproof) My dear child, Mr. Wilberforce is my governor. Mr. Wilberforce is one of the heads of East India House. Mr. Wilberforce looked on the King as his only equal. Now they've put the old boy in that room with the soft walls, Mr. Wilberforce has to fall back on God.
Fanny: Poor Mr. Wilberforce. He must be so lonely.
Charles: Mr. Wilberforce is so lonely that he must keep his employees with him fifteen hours of every day. Mr. Wilberforce can boast that no clerk of his ever fell asleep at his ledgers.

Mr. Wilberforce has insured against stolen repose by provid-
ing stools of such giddy height that a fall may well prove
fatal. May God damn Mr. Wilberforce!

Fanny: In that case Mr. Wilberforce would have no one to
talk to.

Charles: He spoke to me only this morning. "Lamb," he said,
"you come late." "Ah," I answered, "but think how early I
leave!"

Fanny: I think Mr. Wilberforce deserves a portrait in one of
your essays.

Charles: It's my curse that I cannot etch in acid.

Fanny: Can you write only of the things you love?

Charles: I cannot do that either. They have not yet made the
words to describe you fittingly.

Fanny: You found some pretty ones for your reviews of my performances. You made me feel I was the most famous actress
in all England.

Charles: You will be, the day after your new play opens. And I
shall continue to be a dusty little clerk on a stool at East
India House.

Fanny: You will continue to be what you are now—a great,
great writer.

Charles: Give me two greats, and what would you have left for
Wordsworth? He starves on less than five.

Fanny: Then he must go hungry. I cannot give them to him.

Charles: Good. Give them to Coleridge.

Fanny: If you say so, Charles. At least five for Coleridge.

Charles: We were made for each other.

(Embraces her)

Fanny: I must go. I must go. Where's my reticule?

(Finds it in a chair near the mantel. She looks at the mantel where she sees two figurines. The figure of a shepherd is
on the right corner; that of a shepherdess on the left corner. She reverses this order)

Ah, look what's happened! After I put them the way they
should be.

(Turning the faces toward each other)

There. Now they are looking at each other.

(Looks around again, goes to table, picks up several tank-

ards and puts them in a cabinet upright. Fanny behaves
like a young housewife)
These belong here.
  (Looking around again)
Charles, I hope your sister will like these.
  (Fanny indicates potted flowers)
They are to welcome her home.
Charles: You were sweet to bring them. You were sweet. They'll
be the first thing she'll see when I fetch her back here.
Fanny: She's made a long visit, hasn't she?
Charles: Y-e-s, a long visit.
Fanny: That must mean she's been having a pleasant time.
Charles: They . . . they are very fond of her where she's been
staying.
Fanny: I want so much for her to like me.
Charles: She must. It's a family failing.
Fanny: Charles, do you think it will be different after your sis-
ter comes home? Perhaps I'd better not come here so often
after today?
Charles: Oh, nonsense, Fanny.
Fanny: (With a sense of foreboding) I hope it's nonsense.
  (A last loving look around the room)
We've been so happy here these weeks. It's been sanctuary.
Charles: It must always be.
  (Enter, from the door to the inner room, George Dyer. He
  is a small, unkempt, almost indistinguishable little man of
  middle years. He walks into the room slowly, a somnam-
  bulist's pace. He is poring over a book with a scholar's intensity. Under his right arm he has several more books.
  Very slowly he goes to the chair, upstage center, and sits
  down. Fanny and Charles watch his entrance with mock
  solemnity. After George is seated, there is a moment's
  silence)
Fanny: Charles, make him stop his infernal din.
Charles: What! Silence George Dyer, God of thunder! You
blasphemer!
  (Enter, door to inner room, Becky. She is a stout, bristling,
  middle-aged maid, obviously too long in the service of the

Lambs. She goes up to the table. After her trips Emma
Isola. She is a girl of twelve, endearing in every way. She
carries a large album)

Charles: (To Becky) Good evening, least pleasing of the
bestals.

Becky: (Disapproving of Fanny's presence) A person would
think you'd be getting ready to go for your sister. Look at
you, not even dressed.

Fanny: (Beginning to move off left) I was going this minute.
Good evening, Becky.

(Becky makes no reply)

Becky: (Standing looking at Dyer with evident displeasure)
Look at him sitting there, silly old heathen.

Emma: (Near the buffet) You said I could help.

Becky: That's what I said. You've been here long enough to
learn to be of use. Put that silly book down and set the
knives and forks straight.

(Turning to Dyer again)
Dyer!

(Charles and Fanny have moved off left by now. Dyer, if
possible, becomes even more placid)

Becky: You!

(Dyer starts)
I told you to put some wood on the fire!

Dyer: Ah yes, Becky, you did, you did. I fear it slipped my
memory.

Becky: Oh, of course, it was all of three minutes ago.

(Dyer rises slowly. Elaborately removes the crescent-
shaped spectacles, puts them in a case and comes help-
lessly forward. Becky brushes by him on her way to fire)
Oh, sit down, useless.

(Dyer does so)
Pinch and scrape,

(Throwing wood on the fire)
and fight the tradesmen and they bring *that* one

(Meaning Dyer)
into the house to give a body more work.

(With a quick look at the buffet table)

Now who's taken the tankards off the table?

    (Goes to the glass cabinet and removes the tankards that
    Fanny placed there)

I thought so!

    (Takes the tankards to the buffet again)

People acting as if they owned the house. Actresses, with
paint on their faces. Thank God, Miss Mary's coming back!
Now he'll stop his goings on.

    (Gives Emma some of the tankards)

Here. Set them

    (Points to positions on the table)

here and here and here the way they were before.

Charles: (Returning from left wing, to Emma, who has moved
    to the fireplace and stands before the portrait of the girl, the
    lamb, and the roses, enraptured) Emma, I am so glad that
    you've come to us. How do you like us here?

Emma: Oh, very much, Mr. Lamb.

Charles: Come, tell me, how do you get on? I've had no chance
    to talk with you since you arrived yesterday.

Becky: You'd have had a chance if you'd met her at the stage-
    coach the way you said you would.

Charles: I know, I know, I'm a miserable sinner. I got the days
    mixed up.

Becky: Writers! Always getting their days mixed up.

    (Back to her grievance)

Poor child, walking here all alone from the stagecoach inn.
Walking alone through the streets of London.

Emma: I loved it. It's so exciting. I never saw so many people.

Becky: (Blood-curdling whisper) Do you know what happens
    to girls who go about the streets alone?

Charles: Becky, for Heaven's sakes don't tell her!

Emma: Please, Mr. Lamb, I'd like to hear.

Becky: There's filthy drunken villains that lie waiting for them
    and they carry them off to the docks and they sell them to
    sailors for wives. Those girls never see England again.

Emma: Oh, mercy!

Becky: There's little enough mercy for those creatures.

Charles: Don't delude the child, Becky.

    (To Emma)

My dear, the streets of London are all the miracles of life.
Let them have their empty country lanes. Let them lean
against their cows and listen to their nightingales. Nightingales! What melody is there to a nightingale's song? How
much sweeter are the London street sounds at night! Isn't
that so, George?

Dyer: (Fumbling his glasses) I fear I was not attending, sir.

Charles: The street sounds . . . London . . . the sounds in the
night. You know, Fire! Stop, thief! Murder!

Dyer: (Rises and in a most considered tone of voice says) I am
conscious that there is a certain amount of restlessness in the
streets in the small hours. However, the sounds are not too
abrasive if the voices are sufficiently far off, and if the words
of their calls are not entirely distinguishable.

Charles: George, you are, as always, perfect.

Dyer: Thank you, but I fear you much exaggerate.
    (He bows and resumes his seat and his reading)
    (Emma giggles at him)

Charles: You find him droll, my dear? You will also find that he
is God Almighty's gentleman.

Emma: Does he read all the time?

Charles: Not all. He also has time to be poet, philosopher,
scholar and an advocate of the cause of the poor of England.

Emma: Oh, he's a writer?

Charles: He is indeed a writer. Who but a fellow writer would
have described Shakespeare as a great but irregular genius?
    (To Becky)
Becky, have you caught sight of my greatcoat?

Becky: God knows where it is. You said you left it at East India
House.

Charles: It wasn't there. I must've left it someplace where I
wanted to be myself.
    (Noticing Emma staring at Dyer)
That's right, my child, admire him. He merits it.
    (Charles goes off through the door to the inner room)

Emma: (To Becky in a hallowed whisper) Then he's famous.
    (As she retrieves her album)
He's famous. He's famous.

Becky: He's a dirty old image!

Emma: Oo!

Becky: He doesn't hear you. He doesn't hear anything.

Emma: But Mr. Lamb just said he was a writer.

Becky: I say he's a worthless old fool. What manner of man
comes in to breakfast last May and is still here in October?
The way people impose on those two innocents! I don't mind
so much for him; it's poor Miss Mary.

   (Noticing the album still clutched to Emma's breast)
What's that book you've got there? You haven't touched any
of the books in this house, have you?

Emma: Oh, no, this is mine. This is my autograph album. I
thought maybe some of the famous people who come here
might inscribe in it.

Becky: Oh, for God's sakes! Now come along, help me here. We
must have the supper laid when Miss Mary comes.
   (Emma puts the album back on top of the book-shelf and
   with another fond look at the portrait over the mantelpiece joins Becky at the buffet)
No, child, set the plates so.

Emma: Wouldn't they be more in the fashion set so?
   (Makes an attempt)

Becky: No, no, no! Remember if you're going to live here
there's to be no changes in this house. Changes overset poor
Miss Lamb.

Emma: Why do you always say "poor" Miss Lamb? Is there
something the matter with her?

Becky: No. Not now.

Emma: (She puts her hand adoringly on one of the glasses on
the table. Note: These are the Hogarth glasses. Each glass
has a print of the series "The Rake's Progress" on it) Oh,
what pretty glasses. They have paintings on them.

Becky: Put that down! Don't you ever touch those glasses.

Emma: (Obeying) Are they so particular?

Becky: They are the Hogarth glasses. Every glass has a different
picture on it. They're on the walls too.
   (Shuddering)
Nasty things, I call them. Pictures ought to be pretty. But
Miss Lamb calls them her treasures—poor dear.

Emma: I do want to help, but you won't let me do anything.

Becky: Well, mind your manners, then. Fetch the cold water jugs from the scullery.

    (Emma exits to the scullery. Becky busies herself at the table)

Dyer: (Sighing, he regretfully turns the last page of his book) I fear I have not been of great assistance.

Becky: The day you'll be of assistance to anyone, I'll never live to see.

    (Emma returns with the water jugs, filled)

Dyer: Ah, the cold water. May I not fetch the brandy to place beside it? I believe I heard Mr. Lamb say cold water's insipid without brandy.

    (Goes up to cabinet, right)

Becky: Thank God, there's something in it. It used to be full every evening, empty every morning. That's the way it used to be.

Emma: Did they drink it all up every night?

Becky: It was no "they." It was a "he."

Dyer: (Protesting) It was long the generous custom on the occasions of their Thursday night gatherings for Miss Mary Lamb and Mr. Charles Lamb to supply brandy and other spirituous beverages for the delectation of their guests. Truly a most hospitable provision.

    (Emma giggles)

Becky: They—generous to their Thursday guests, and me haggling Thursday and every other day to bring the bills down a ha'penny. Thursday nights! All the people, all the talking, the drinking and the smoking. It was no good for poor Miss Lamb. I hope they'll stay away from now on and let her rest; her so long from home this last time.

Emma: Is Miss Lamb often from home?

Becky: Not as often as they say.

    (Dyer is in her way)

    Will you sit down and read your book?

Dyer: I have but a few moments since completed the reading of my book.

Becky: Then go read it again.

Dyer: A splendid notion! I perhaps scampered too lightly over
its surface.

(Sits and resumes reading)

Emma: (To Dyer) Would you inscribe in my album?

(Charles overhears her as he re-enters)

Dyer: I would be more than pleased, young lady, but unfortu-
nately I have lost the use of these two fingers,

(Extends the second and third finger of his left hand)

due to copying out the manuscript of the New Testament in
a fine Greek hand.

Charles: George, I should find it impossible to live without
you. Why don't you copy out the manuscript of your poems?

Dyer: I've left off poesies, sir, in favor of a more urgent work. I
am about to embark upon my autobiography again. The
world must await the publication of my poems for another
year or two.

Charles: George, if I could calculate the precise date of your
death, I would write a novel on purpose to make you the
hero. God bless you, George, and God bless all your works.
You're the only literary character I've ever been happily acquainted with.

(Emma, seeing that Dyer is not going to inscribe, turns to
Charles, who takes the book)

Emma: Mr. Lamb, won't you?

Charles: (He flips the pages) Why, what a relief! The pages are
blank. You have some plan for filling them?

Emma: Oh, yes! It's for people's autographs.

Charles: People?

Emma: Well, only famous people, of course.

Charles: (Returning it to her quickly) Good God!

Emma: (Bubbling happily) So I thought . . . Thursday nights
here when all the famous people come—we've heard about
Thursday nights, even down in the country—and I
thought . . .

(Charles moves away and she follows him repeating each
of the following names as she turns a page)

Mr. Wordsworth . . . Mr. Southey . . . Mr. Hazlitt . . . Mr.
Leigh Hunt . . .

Charles: For writers to be fleeced by their publishers at least

has the comfortable dignity of tradition. But this—exploita-
tion by amateurs!

Emma: (Finishing) And even Mr. Coleridge.

Charles: You want the greatest one of all, my dear.

Emma: Does he come often?

Charles: I don't dare think how long it's been since I've seen
him.

Emma: Isn't he in London?

Charles: I don't know. Wherever. I'm afraid Coleridge is off in
some howling world of his own. His world of broken hopes,
torn promises, and the quick deceits of laudanum.

Emma: Oh, mercy, does Mr. Coleridge drink laudanum?

Dyer: He was ordered the drug for the relief of his pain. It is
said that the pangs of rheumatic fever are almost beyond
endurance.

Charles: Oh, George! That rheumatic fever was when he was
fourteen years old. No, the fever is no longer of his body.
   (To Emma)
My dear, if you could only have seen him when we were
schoolmates together at Christ's Hospital. He was not a human, he was a . . .
   (Scrambles for the right word)
an archangel. But those days are gone. There's a white stone
over them. Oh, let him forget himself if he can but he should
not forget his friends.

Dyer: I believe, sir, that Mr. Coleridge has no more forgotten
you and your sister than you have forgotten him. I believe
there is far less sin in human beings than is ascribed to them.

Charles: (To Emma) You see, there is the kindliest heart that
God ever put into human flesh.
   (Becky, who has been busy in and out of the scullery, is on
   during the reading of this line)
As, no doubt, our most Christian housekeeper has
mentioned.

Emma: She said Mr. Dyer was a . . . a rather frequent visitor.

Charles: A visitor since April last or was it August? No matter.
It was a Tuesday breakfast time when he scrambled up to our
door prepared to die. We found he was starved, that's all. He
had given all his money away to his relatives. No man ever

had so many dirty little nieces and nephews. So here he stays, thank God, and we endeavor to feed him once a day anyway. A shilling each night for his dinner, and we take it from him. If we didn't, it would go all over the world.

Dyer: (During the latter part of Charles' speech, removes glasses, starts a systematic, thoroughly fruitless search through his pockets) I must ask you to excuse me, I find I have misplaced my coin.

    (Bows solemnly, goes off through door to inner chambers)

Charles: Doubtless left his shilling in his water jug. Now he will reach his room and probably forget what he went there for and certainly forget to return. Head uniformly wrong, heart uniformly right.

    (Goes to buffet, starts pouring a drink of porter)

Becky: Still no brandy?

Charles: Still malt beverages.

    (He raises the glass, stops, inspects it closer, and then wheels on Becky)

I have told you *never* to put this glass out where my sister might see it.

Becky: I can't tell one of those things from another.

Charles: There'll be no danger of that anymore!

    (Goes to fireplace and smashes the glass)

Emma: Oh, Mr. Lamb, Becky said they are Miss Lamb's treasures.

Charles: They are. All but that one.

Emma: What was that one?

Charles: The picture on that glass was one of Bedlam.

    (He walks back to the buffet and pours another glass of porter. There is a knock on the door. Charles forces a gaiety)

What! Some nocturnal guests?

    (The knock repeats)

Or rather knock-eternal guests.

    (Becky goes off to answer the door; the pun is unnoticed)

Oh, come, the best puns are the worst ones.

    (Shrugs)

Oh, well, try it again later.

    (Enter Coleridge from left wing, followed by Becky who

goes off to the scullery. Coleridge is not a handsome man,
but he is arresting. There is a carelessness in his attire, a
mark of preoccupation. Though heavily built he is not
much taller than Charles. As he enters, he is at his worst;
shaken, haggard, jittery)

Coleridge: (Cries out desperately) Charles!

Charles: Coleridge!

(They embrace)

Are you all right?

Coleridge: (Groans his reply) And how are you?

Charles: (Groans) Where in God's name have you been?

Coleridge: In hell, at various addresses. Tell me, Charles, your
sister—is she here?

Charles: Mary is coming back today, thank God. They sent me
word she's well. I'm going to fetch her.

(Emma, once realizing who Coleridge is, makes a dive for
her album and comes up to them)

This is Emma. Emma Isola. And this, my child, is the
mighty Coleridge.

(Becky appears from the scullery, goes to the table)

Coleridge: Is she related to you?

Charles: She is sadly off but not that sadly. Emma was mother-
less and her father lately died. Mary could not bear the
thought of her becoming a public ward, so she has come to
live with us. She will bring the primroses into this house of
winter.

Coleridge: (To Charles) Surely there are others who are better
situated to shelter this child!

Emma: (To Coleridge) Miss Lamb isn't here now but she's coming home today. Coming back to live.

Coleridge: Oh, I've missed Mary. I've needed her. It will be like
touching earth again to see her. I think she is my sister, too.

Charles: I think she's a sister to all the world.

Coleridge: How long has she been from home?

Charles: Since last you saw her.

Coleridge: Oh, my God! That long.

Charles: I have not counted the weeks. And the violence, this
time, increased.

Emma: (With her album to Coleridge) Please, sir.

Becky: Emma, you come here and help me.

(Becky takes Emma into the scullery)

Coleridge: I blame myself. I blame myself for what has happened. I brought a guest here. He said he so admired Mary. He said he wanted to see her. God, how was I to know the cursed fool had known your mother? And he talked to Mary about your mother. And he talked and talked and talked about your mother. Stories about her . . . Questions about her . . . And I couldn't stop him. I couldn't shut his damned mouth.

Charles: I should've been here. I should have guarded her. But I was lying with my head on a tavern table.

Coleridge: I brought the blundering idiot here. I brought him. I blame myself.

Charles: There is no blame to you, Coleridge. No one can foresee these things. We try to protect her. We keep incessant watch lest Mother be mentioned in her presence. But it sometimes happens. It happens and the dreadful harm is done. Oh, there are other causes, too, and we are prone to blame the one nearest at hand. It might be fatigue, or the excitement of company, or it might be talk of Bedlam, or it need be no excuse at all.

Coleridge: God, I can't forget her as I last saw her. The look on her face. That slow ominous smile. I knew I must hurry. I got a hackney coach and took her to the nursing home.

Charles: While I lay stupefied.

Coleridge: At first she was quite calm and told me what must be done. Then she began crying wildly. Oh, I was cut to the heart.

Charles: I know. You know what she means to me.

Coleridge: I know what she means to all of us. She gives us strength. I need strength. I'm weak.

Charles: Oh, that day of horrors. The day that Mary's madness first seized her and she did murder. Years and years she had worked and strained taking care of all of us. Taking care of me. Her life was toil and sacrifice and rebuff; no life at all. She had so much love to give and none to take it. There was no refuge for her heart. How often have I seen her come to my mother not for praise, not for endearments, but only to be granted some small sign that she existed. My mother was a good mother but not to a daughter. And the day came, may God Almighty have us all in His keeping, when Mary's mind broke. I was home in time to see my mother's dead and murdered corpse and to take the knife from my sister's hand. Oh, Coleridge, I've never spoken of that day to anyone but you . . .

Coleridge: I know, Charles.

Charles: All London knew . . . The public papers . . . We were marked people. I am always in terror of what will become of Mary, of how I am to take care of her. Oh, Coleridge, I need money.

Coleridge: Doesn't your brother John aid you?

Charles: John! I had to go on my knees to John to borrow money for Mary's care this time. God knows he is the last man I'd go to for money, but I had no choice. He never eases. He has been trying to break me down ever since the day the magistrate paroled Mary in my care. He would have her thrown in Bedlam and kept there. So long as I live, so help me God, that will not happen!

Coleridge: When she is not ill, her mind is the sanest I know. Perhaps the only sane mind I know.

Charles: She is so deeply fond of you, Coleridge, that I beg of you to be careful with her when she comes home. She worries about you. She knows what wild things you have done and she dreads what that damned stuff may make you do next.

Coleridge: I will be careful.

Charles: Coleridge, you will wait for Mary, won't you? It will give her such joy to see you.

Coleridge: Yes, of course, I'll wait.

Charles: (Calling Becky inside) Becky!

(To Coleridge)

I'll set our dragon to guard you.

(Becky enters)

Mr. Coleridge will wait until I bring my sister back. Will you take steps to make him comfortable?

Becky: (To Coleridge) You'd best go within, there's a decent fire there. Not that that Dyer had anything to do with it.

Coleridge: Anywhere, anywhere.

Becky: (To Charles) And see that the poor lady wraps up well.
  It's raw in the streets.

Charles: I will bring her in a hackney coach.

  (Emma enters; goes right to Charles. He embraces her)
  I'll soon be back with my sister, my child. Now don't let
  Becky intimidate you too much. Myself, she has me in a con-
  stant state of cringe.

  (Charles exits left)

Emma: (Turns brightly to Becky) What can I do?

Becky: You can stay out of the way.

  (Emma comes downstage to table, left, and assists her in
  taking off the cover of the table)

Emma: Oo, all the paper and quills.

  (Picks up a sheet of paper)
  Is this Mr. Lamb's writing? Is it a book?

Becky: It's not. It's the writing they're doing together, and you
  put it down. You're not to touch a thing, you hear? Everything is to be just the way it was before Miss Lamb went
  from home.

Emma: Is she often from home?

Becky: Not as often as they say.

  (Becky is folding the cover now. The child turns back toward the fireplace and the portrait of the child, the lamb,
  and the roses)

Emma: Isn't that a dear little lamb?

Becky: I suppose so.

Emma: Who is the little girl? Is that Miss Lamb when she was
  little?

Becky: No, it isn't.

Emma: Is it her mother?

Becky: (Her eyes go to the ceiling) Oh, dear God, here it
  comes! No, child, it's a picture that belonged to Miss Lamb's
  grandmother.

Emma: Did you know her?

Becky: No, I didn't.

Emma: Do you know Miss Lamb's mother?

Becky: Yes, I did.

Emma: Is she a lovely lady?

Becky: She was if she liked you.

Emma: Where is she?

Becky: She isn't anywhere. Now will you for God's sakes stop your silly questions.

Emma: Is she in heaven, like my mother?

Becky: I told you to stop asking me questions.

Emma: Well, then I'll ask Miss Lamb when she comes.

Becky: You listen to me, Miss. If I ever catch you asking Miss Lamb anything about her mother, you know what I'll do to you?

Emma: (Whispering) What will you do?

Becky: I'll take you like this—

    (Gets Emma by the shoulders)

and I'll shake you like this—

    (Shakes Emma)

and like this

    (Increases)

and like this

    (Increases)

and I'll go on shaking you and shaking you and shaking you . . .

Curtain

End of Scene 1

ACT ONE : SCENE 2

Time: A little while later.

Scene: The curtain rises on a vacant stage. In a moment
  Charles enters and takes a position near the working table,
  downstage left. Mary slowly enters. She is not a beautiful
  woman—she is a lovely woman. She has dignity without se-
  verity; calm without lethargy. She has no spite, no mean-
  ness, and all who come near her feel welcome. As she enters
  the room, slowly rediscovering it after her absence, she is
  exalted. Each article in the room is a source of joy to her.
  She moves about the room, picking up a glass here, a piece of
  silverware there; all of the associations she has had are reverently and joyfully recalled.

Mary: I'm so glad. I'm so glad. Oh, Charles, it's as if I'd left
  this room but ten minutes ago.
  (Shaking her head as she again reviews the room)
  There have been no changes. Everything is in its same place.
  (She moves downstage, toward Charles)
  Everything's the same.
  (She arrives at the worktable)
  But, oh, not here. Oh, not our worktable. Where are the
  crumpled papers, the splashes of ink? Where are the quills
  you break in despair when the right words won't come from
  them? Oh, Charles, I'm afraid this is all much too tidy.
Charles: It is true that I have not been setting down many
  words, but after all, that is merely a manual matter. My
  thoughts have not lain fallow. Thought, dear Mary, has its
  seasons and mine is at its Springtime. The tender buds are
  nigh to burst into rich heavy blossoms.
Mary: "Tender buds?" "Rich heavy blossoms?" Charles, what in
  God's name is all this botany? The excuses I've heard for no
  work; but "buds" and "blossoms" . . .
Charles: I expect I need you sitting across the worktable
  from me.
Mary: I shall be there now. We'll work again.
  (Turning back to review the room)
  Oh, it's so good to be home.

(Noticing the potted flowers)

And you got me flowers, Charles. It's so long since I've seen flowers growing. Thank you.

Charles: Mary, I didn't—

Mary: Why, it's the way you used to bring me posies when you were a little boy.

Charles: Mary, it was Fanny Kelly who brought them. She wanted them to speak a welcome to you.

Mary: Oh. Oh, that was most thoughtful, wasn't it? She must be a dear girl.

Becky: (Enters slowly. She adores Mary) Oh, Miss Mary, welcome home!

Mary: Oh, Becky, I'm glad to see you.

Becky: You look well.

Mary: I am well. All well. You've kept the house beautifully; everything's right.

Becky: I knew you would want things just as they were.

Mary: I have thought and thought of this room. I've remembered everything about it. It's all the same way it was . . . no, no, there's something . . .

(Her hands go to head, a gesture of concentration and recollection)

There's something . . . *something's* different. Ah, of course.

(She goes to the mantel)

Somebody's changed them around.

(She indicates the two figurines. Becky exchanges looks with Charles. Mary speaks gently)

Who's done this to my little shepherd and shepherdess? My Corydon and Phyllis? I don't want them smirking at each other.

(She changes their positions, turning them so that they face away from each other)

(To Becky)

Becky, have you taken good care of George Dyer?

Becky: He's fed and dusted.

Emma: (Entering in a rush) Miss Mary. Miss Mary.

Mary: It makes my homecoming sweeter to find you here. I have so many plans for our good times together.

Emma: Mr. Lamb said that you would teach me Latin.

Charles: She's much too pretty ever to be a good Latin scholar.

Mary: Of course I'll teach you—and perhaps my brother will teach you botany.

(She gives Emma a loving caress)

Charles: I can wait no longer! There's a surprise for you here.

(He calls through the door)

Oh, Maestro! Mary's home.

(Coleridge enters)

Mary: (Delighted) Coleridge!

Coleridge: (Embraces her) Mary! I've needed you so much. You've never looked better.

Mary: (After a quick study) Ah, dear Coleridge, *you* have.

Charles: He needs rest.

Coleridge: I need friendship more.

Mary: You'll find them both here with us.

Becky: Miss Mary, you mustn't get over-tired. Come inside and have a nice lie-down and rest.

Mary: I'm quite well, Becky. I don't need a rest. But I will go take off my bonnet and change this heavy gown. Coleridge, promise not to vanish.

Coleridge: I promise.

(Mary, Becky, and Emma exit through door to the inner room)

My God, Charles, she looks radiant.

Charles: She is a strong woman.

Coleridge: I envy her strength. I have none; I'm weak. I'm afraid. I'm afraid to be seen. I'm afraid to see people. I'm afraid even to ask for people.

Charles: (Cheering up Coleridge) I'll tell you without the asking. Things go quietly along their natural course. Leigh Hunt is still in prison for the crime of attacking the Prince Regent in writing.

(Ruefully)

I'm still at liberty for the want of a sharp enough quill.

Coleridge: Hunt still imprisoned?

Charles: Yes. His life has become so usual to him there that his wife, who shares his cell, is again heavy with child. His paper, "The Examiner," goes on somehow. I wish to God it hadn't. In the black night of remorse, after Mary's seizure, I wrote a piece for them—a Confession. It's a filthy fashion, this rage for publishing one's degradations. Today a writer has a single collision with the normal world, and he makes a whole book of his personal damages.

Coleridge: Has your piece been published yet?

Charles: The readers loved it. They ate it up.

Coleridge: What was its title?

Charles: "Confessions of a Drunkard."

Coleridge: Oh, Christ, Charles! Has Mary seen it?

Charles: No. Oh, God, no, Coleridge! You know how my drinking torments her. I take only malt beverages now. It's a late atonement to her. Well, let's see, what other news? Well, you knew that Mary and I contracted to do a book of stories of Shakespeare's plays, designed to interest children. God, what one will do for a guinea!

Coleridge: How far have you come with the book?

Charles: Oh, perhaps midway. You see, I've been waiting for Mary. It wasn't entirely the guinea. It is healthful for Mary to work together with me. It's long since she's tried her own writing. It's long since she's tried anything alone. And I, well, work is easier when she's with me.

(Sighs)

I've written an occasional piece and signed it "Elia"—that name I stole from a fellow clerk. But after days at that damned East India House, I have little time and less heart for writing. But I must make more money. If you knew what regular money would mean to me. It would mean that Mary would always be cared for. It would mean an end to anxiety. It would mean freedom. It would mean—Fanny Kelly.

(Coleridge looks surprised)

Yes, I have seen what happiness could be. Oh, it's torment to see it right there before you and not be able to reach out your hand and take it. I want to marry her.

Coleridge: You! You want to domesticate?

Charles: I want nothing else in life. I want to live like other men. Like happy men, like well men.

Coleridge: So that's why no brandy? Less an atonement to Mary than an offering to Miss Kelly. Does Miss Kelly know what you are giving up?

Charles: No. Only a part of it. Only a part of what I've had to fight.

Coleridge: Oh, then she was not among the readers who ate up "Confessions of a Drunkard"?

Charles: For God's sakes, no, Coleridge.

Coleridge: I see. Does Mary know about her?

Charles: Mary knows who she is, of course; everybody does. And coming home in the coach I found myself talking of no one else.

Coleridge: Does Mary know the true state of your feeling?

Charles: I'll tell her presently. I cannot risk anything too sudden.

Coleridge: I see.

Charles: (He goes to table, pours a glass of porter, lifts the glass in a toast)

Well, to Fanny Kelly.

(Mary re-enters, in a change. She cannot help but over-hear the Fanny Kelly toast. Charles is somewhat uncomfortable about it)

Mary: M'm, a toast to Miss Kelly? And in malt beverage? Why, Charles—

(She pats his shoulder fondly)

how original is her effect upon you!

(Mary moves to cabinet where the Hogarth glasses are stationed)

Ah, my Hogarth glasses!

(Turning to Coleridge)

Now, Col, tell us about you? Where have you been?

Coleridge: Anywhere, as far and as fast as I could go. But never far enough nor fast enough to leave my cursed self behind.

Mary: But your family?

Charles: Your wife is no doubt well?

Coleridge: (Dryly) My wife is no doubt well.

Mary: And what of your friends?

Coleridge: I've not even heard of them.

Mary: Charles wrote me what news there was. My brother's an angel—a letter every day.

Coleridge: What about Burnett? And Lloyd? How's Dyer?

Charles: Dyer's the same. Possibly a shade more dusty.

Mary: It's a comfort to have him living with us.

Coleridge: Oh, you and Charles cannot shelter the world.

Charles: Save Dyer, it seems most of our playfellows are literally on the town. Let me see, Burnett is excellently situated in debtors' prison. Fenwicke occupies a like estate.

Mary: His wife and children dwell in charity on the parish.

Charles: Farr's gone off to the workhouse again. Hazlitt left his wife for his landlady's daughter.

Mary: His landlady's daughter then left him for somebody else.

Charles: So now Hazlitt goes about bearing his frustrate love like a blazing torch.

Coleridge: And Wordsworth?

Charles: (Dryly) Your god, Wordsworth?

Coleridge: The giant, Wordsworth, God love him.

Mary: (Patting Coleridge on the shoulder) My dear, we do not attempt to direct the affections of the Almighty.

Charles: Wordsworth is, as usual, up to his rump in sunsets.

Coleridge: (To Mary) Charles says that you are working on the Shakespeare book. That's good news.

Mary: It would be better news for poor Charles if I could spell. He says if there are possibly two ways to spell a word I will find a third.

Coleridge: What have you done so far? "Lear"? "Hamlet"? "Macbeth"?

Mary: (Charles shakes his head warningly at Coleridge) I am doing only the comedies. Charles fears the tragedies are too . . . unpleasant for me.

Charles: I do the tragedies. The tragedies, most of the grammar, and all the spelling are mine.

Coleridge: Oh, I've missed hearing of people working.

Charles: (Bitterly) But have you missed hearing of people slaving? It goes on—day and night—at East India House.

Mary: It's so hard for him. He is so good about it, so brave.

Coleridge: Charles, how long have you been there?

Charles: Since I was fourteen years old. An even thousand years.

Coleridge: How close are you to your pension?

Charles: About as close as to Heaven.

Mary: The directors of East India House, like the directors of
   Heaven, must take your life before they give you your
   reward.
Charles: Well, fortunately, there are some rewards for the
   living. Coleridge is back; that's one of them. We have
   missed you.
Coleridge: I've missed you. I've missed London.
Charles: The whole town's waiting for you. The streets, the
   book-sellers, the galleries—
Coleridge: London!
   (Fondly)
   How good that it all sounds the same!
Mary: But they tell me there's something new. It's now the
   fashion to have tea at Bedlam of a Sunday.
   (She bursts out)
   They go there to laugh at the poor mad wretches chained to
   their beds naked. And some day they will come there and
   look at me! And they'll laugh at my shaved head, and they'll
   throw me bits of their cakes! Because that's where I'll be!
   That's where I'll end my days! That's where—
Charles: (Softly) Mary, you must stop that.
Mary: Thank you, Charles. I'm sorry, Coleridge.
   (Pulling herself together)
Charles: The theater, Coleridge—that awaits you, too. There's
   an excitement to Drury Lane that lifts the heart!
Mary: (To Coleridge) The excitement is named Miss Fanny
   Kelly.
Coleridge: Yes. Charles told me about her.
Mary: I am sure he did. He told me, too, all the way home.
   I've seen her, of course, at Drury Lane. I cannot wait to
   know her.
Charles: What an actress!
Mary: Charles wrote a while ago in his review of her that she
   was a lass to go a-gypsying through the world with.
Coleridge: You couldn't go a-gypsying past Picadilly Circus.
Charles: I'm not at all sure that I couldn't.
Mary: There was one time he went a-gypsying away from Lon-
   don and found himself in the village stocks for drunkenness.
Charles: I was just a lad.

Mary: You were thirty-four at the time.

Coleridge: Is Miss Kelly so beautiful?

Charles: A plain divine face.

Mary: Yes, that phrase was in Charles' review, too. Mr. Wordsworth calls it one of the teardrops of literature. I did not think all that highly of it myself.

Coleridge: And shall I meet this lovely lady?

Mary: I think we may expect to see her quite often.

Charles: It can't be often. She cannot often enough slip away from that merciless jailer, her mother. The infernal, prying old bitch . . .

Mary: Why, Charles!

Charles: Ministers of grace, defend us from the mothers of actresses!

Mary: That's a matter for St. Jude, my dear. He specializes in lost causes. There, there.

(She takes Charles' hand affectionately. To Coleridge)
Do you think Charles looks well?

Coleridge: Passably.

Mary: (With utmost calm) Remember how he used to sit up till dawn on flattery and gin and water? How well he looked? Now there's a change come over him. You see he takes no spirits. Becky tells me he is in bed by midnight, and he looks like the very Devil himself. A strange man, my brother.

Charles: (Changing the subject) Coleridge, how is your little son?

Coleridge: I'm told he's thriving.

Mary: Does he more resemble you or his mother?

Coleridge: I wouldn't know.

Mary: Dear Coleridge, there's something that Charles and I have long wanted to talk to you about.

(Coleridge is uneasy, resistant)

Charles: (Softening it a little for Coleridge's sake) Well, perhaps not wanted to, but—

Mary: We *must* talk to you about it, Coleridge. Your wife— have you written to her?

Charles: Coleridge, you should write to her.

Coleridge: (Bitterly to Charles) And you, Brutus.

(To Mary)

I am so miserable, I dare not encounter her. I know it's deplorable. I respect her greatly and I cannot stand her.

Mary: Don't say it. We allow in full force everything you can feel or think. But do not say it.

Charles: I do not allow it in full force! He's got everything in the world. He's got what other men would give an arm for. He's got a wife and a home and a child and a life.

Mary: (Slowly) Oh, yes; oh, yes. I said a change had come over him. Even while I was saying it, I did not fully understand.

Coleridge: (Thinking the remark for himself) But you have always understood. You have the fairest of minds.

Mary: (Sadly) Sometimes.

Coleridge: I am told that my wife goes on very well.

Mary: Yes, I know. They say she is fat and happy. They say that *I* am fat and happy, too. Coleridge, to give another pain is to give yourself worse pain. Can't you see that your secrecy means suffering for both her and you? Secrecy is such cruel conduct. Two people who are bound together must share life as Charles and I have done. We tell each other everything that happens. Where we go, what we do, we exchange opinions, we hide nothing. After all, it's the only groundwork of companionship.

Coleridge: All right! I will! I will! Tomorrow!

Mary: We know your "tomorrow."

Charles: (Derisively) Yes, "tomorrow." And you'll give up that damned stuff too—"tomorrow."

Mary: Coleridge, are you still . . . ? Do you still . . . ?

Coleridge: If you're trying to ask me if I still drink laudanum, well, I do.

Mary: Oh, I worry so about you.

(Her hands to her temples in despair)

I feel my poor brains go hot in my skull when I think of you.

Coleridge: Oh, Mary, no. I feel low enough.

Charles: (As Mary nods sympathetically to Charles, he goes toward the liquor cabinet with a sudden brightness) I had the rare good fortune of buying a bottle of fine brandy. A brandy too good for the Bonaparte. I've been drinking only porter these past weeks. But this—

(To Coleridge)

the Prodigal's return—

(He pours three glasses of brandy)

Come on, Coleridge. This is such stuff as toasts are made on.

Coleridge: (As Mary takes a glass, he takes one, reluctantly)
To any change. It must be for the better.

Charles: Oh, no. Not like that.

Coleridge: Yes, you're right. When we say the worst has happened, the gods reach for another thunderbolt.

Charles: (Bantering) Oh, come on. I was only trying to lighten your melancholy. Drink up, Prince Hamlet.

Coleridge: (Pushes the glass away savagely. He breaks under the strain of Lamb's "advice") Oh, stop it! What are you trying to do, make fun of me? I thought in this house I was safe from mockery!

Charles: What the Devil's the matter with you?

Coleridge: You know what's the matter with me. You know I can't stop it.

Charles: Yes, you can.

Coleridge: Don't you think I want to? Don't you think I've tried?

Mary: You must want to again and try to again.

Charles: You're too good for this. It's too rotten a waste—

Coleridge: Oh, please!

Mary: You're not just destroying yourself, Coleridge. We never do things just to ourselves. There's your wife and your child.

Charles: God, if I had a wife and child!

(Mary looks at Charles after his outbreak)

Coleridge: Oh, for Heaven's sakes, stop badgering me!

(To Mary)

Let me alone, damn you!

Charles: Don't speak to Mary that way.

Coleridge: Well, I'm sorry but I came here for peace. God, I might just as well be back with the poet laureate. Southey and that damned bird chorus of his.

(Mimics viciously)

"Oh, Coleridge, why don't you at least try? . . . Why don't you pull yourself together? . . . Why don't you behave like other people? . . ." Nya. Nya. Nya. Nya. Nya.

Mary: But they're right! The damned bird chorus is right.
   They're the good people. They're unmarked. Oh, it would be
   so wonderful not to be marked, not to be different.
Coleridge: (Goaded to the breaking point) All right! For
   Christ's gentle sake, all right!
      (He puts a laudanum vial on the table. There is a silence
      as they realize to the full the extent of Coleridge's sacri-
      fice. Charles takes the vial of laudanum from the table,
      walks slowly to the mantelpiece, and places it in the
      center)
      (Through his teeth)
   And I mean it!
Mary: (Moves Coleridge to the writing table) You make us
   very happy. Now, the letter. Paper and quills here. Go on.
Coleridge: Yes, Mary.
      (Sits at the writing table and prepares to write)
      (Becky and Emma re-enter from the scullery. They are
      busy about the room, and noisy)
Emma: (Seeing Coleridge at the table, she goes to Charles and
   whispers) Is he . . . ? Is Mr. Coleridge writing?
Charles: Yes, my dear.
Emma: O-o-o, is it a book?
Charles: Not quite, my child.
      (As Emma moves close to Coleridge)
   Best not hover too close to him, nut brown maiden, he might
   mistake you for his muse. And I doubt if that would
   amuse you.
Emma: (Giggling) Oo, Mr. Lamb.
Mary: Even your puns haven't changed.
Coleridge: (Throws down the quill in a temper) The inkwell's
   dry. The quill's broke! Mary, I'm not meant to write.
Becky: Supper in about an hour, Miss Lamb?
Mary: Very good, Becky. The table looks inviting. Is the bread
   fresh?
Becky: God knows it ought to be. They've raised the price tup-
   pence more.
Mary: Let us see.
      (She takes the bread knife in her hand as if to cut the loaf
      but she stops, transfixed at the sight of the blade)

Charles: Becky!

Becky: (Duty-bound to take the blade from Mary) Please.
Please, Ma'am.

Mary: (Wearied) Oh, Becky.

   (Relinquishes it. To Emma's curious stare)

   You see, child, once I did a terrible thing with a knife.

   (Mary moves, with a tray, left)

Emma: (Hounding Becky) What'd she do, what'd she do,
   what'd she do?

   (Becky gives her a slap and takes her off to the scullery)

Coleridge: Oh, Mary, can't I have quiet?

Mary: Of course, you can, Col.

Charles: You know my desk. I'll lead you there.

   (Charles takes Coleridge off to inner room)

   (Charles returns)

Mary: Charles, you mustn't take quite so much care of me. If
   you treat me as if I were ill—I'll be ill again.

Charles: I'm not treating you any way, Mary, except as one
   treats the other one who comes back home.

Mary: Back home—home together.

   (Tenderly)

   Oh, poor Charles, I'm so conscious of the worry and depression I've caused you. I'm so guilty for taking all your time.

Charles: You give it back to me, doubled in value. And when
   you are the way you are now, you're my prop and mainstay.

Mary: It is you, Charles, that fortifies me. God knows, there
   should be a sweeter purpose to your life.

   (Switching the subject)

   Charles, what did you say before about Fanny Kelly's
   mother?

Charles: That she is an infernal, prying old bitch. Asking what
   rent we pay, trying to find out my salary.

   (He mocks her)

   "And does he expect a pension? And when will it be? And
   how much? And how much does an 'Elia' essay bring in?"

Mary: Whom does she ask?

Charles: Any one. If she cannot find it in the parlor, she'll go
   straight to the scullery. She's as unscrupulous as a . . . a . . .
   a . . .

Mary: (Gently teasing) As a mother-in-law?
   (Charles is uneasy at her perception, but Mary smiles
   reassuringly)
   Oh, I want you to be happy, Charles. Fanny must be very
   lovely, mustn't she?
   (Sadly)
   And she's so young, so young.
Charles: She lends me gaiety.
Mary: Yes, I see. You've had excitement from our friends, and
   companionship, I hope, from me, but you've never known
   gaiety before. Oh, yes, I see.
   (She speaks to herself, declaring a solemn vow)
   I am resolved with all the force of my mind that I will con-
   quer my fears. I will lose them.
Charles: (Puzzled) What fears, Mary?
Mary: Old fears. Too old to be, in any decency, still alive.
   (There is a knock on the door. Charles answers it and re-
   turns with Fanny Kelly)
Charles: Mary, this is Fanny come to welcome you home.
Mary: (Looking at Fanny, says almost to herself) Oh, yes. Oh,
   yes.
Fanny: Oh, Miss Lamb, finally I meet you. Did you have an
   agreeable visit with your friends?
Mary: (With a look at Charles) They were most kind to me.
   We were just speaking about you, Miss Kelly.
Charles: If speaking about her would bring her, she would
   never be absent.
Mary: And your flowers. They are almost as sweet as you are.
Fanny: I'm so glad that you liked them.
Mary: It was good of you to bring me flowers that grow. I cannot bear to see them cut and watch them die. Some day, perhaps, I'll have my own garden. Our little English gardens,
   how good they are. And those who walk among their
   flowers—they're good, too. There's nothing different about
   them.
Charles: You're back sooner than we dared hope. The rehearsal
   went so smoothly?
Fanny: They are doing such things to the play that the author
   weeps.

Charles: The daily exercise of authors. You, yourself, like the piece?

Fanny: I do, indeed! I'm onstage for the entire five acts. Mrs. Siddons worries if I am quite ready to play so demanding a role.

Charles: Mrs. Siddons worries—shall we end the sentence there?

Fanny: I worry, too. I wish there would be better plays. Miss Lamb, why don't you make Mr. Lamb write a play?

Charles: I did once. It had a roaring run of one night.

Mary: In spite of all our friends in the audience, the hisses drowned out the applause.

Charles: Hisses always do. They come more deeply from the heart.

Fanny: Oh, no! They couldn't hiss a play of Mr. Lamb's.

Charles: They could indeed, and I joined in the hissing. I was so damnably afraid of being taken for the author.

Fanny: (To Mary) Oh, make Mr. Lamb write for the theater!

Mary: It is a point of conscience with me never to try to make him do anything. Just because women have better judgment, we have no reason to be tyrants.

Fanny: Mother says men are no better than little children and it's our place to watch them every second.

Charles: And, oh! Does she watch!

Fanny: (A little spat begins) Well, I'm simply telling you what she says, Charles.

(Mary notices the use of Charles' first name)

Charles: I could repeat her every word—backwards, if required.

Fanny: Well, you don't have to be like that, Charles.

Charles: Be like what? I'm not being like anything.

Mary: "Not being like anything"? I think you're being very much like something, Charles.

(She crosses over to Fanny, and takes her hand)

Charles: (Looking at the two women) Well, I'm damned!
(He stalks off)

Fanny: (As Charles goes off) Charles, don't—
(To Mary)
Oh, what must you think of me. You must be shocked.

Mary: No, not that. It's only I had not quite realized that you
two were on such good terms as to be on such bad terms.
(Mary plays this scene with all her warmth and generosity. She is truly anxious for Charles and Fanny's happiness; everything she says is true. She succeeds pretty well
in hiding the pain in her heart, but it is there; for fear of
what must happen when her brother goes from her)

Fanny: It's dreadful that we do this to each other. It must be—
oh, I don't know, nervousness, fatigue, false living . . .
Charles and I—we're not the sort of people who can do this.
We cannot hide and steal and sneak our bits of time we have
together. Everyone should know; everyone ought to see how
proud I am.

Mary: Ah, you *are* in love, aren't you?

Fanny: (She catches herself; she has said too much) Oh, I
didn't mean . . .
(Simply and dependently)
Please, forgive me. I cannot help myself.

Mary: My dear, what have I to forgive? Do you think I could
blame you for loving my brother?

Fanny: Oh, you're so generous, Miss Lamb.

Mary: My name is Mary, my dear.

Fanny: Oh, I'd love to but I don't quite dare. And yet—I cannot make you a stranger.

Mary: No, you mustn't. This isn't really strange. I think I've
long known that it must happen. I think I've always known
it should happen. I can only be thankful that it happened
with you.

Fanny: Oh, if only everybody could understand like you. My
mother—she's in such a state about it.

Mary: What is it that troubles her?
(Alarmed)
Is it . . . is it something about me?

Fanny: Oh, no, Miss Lamb, what could there be about you? It's
Charles; it's Mr. Lamb. She doesn't want us to be—"us." You
see, my mother distrusts people who aren't like everyone
else. People that are poets and artists and writers . . .

Mary: What does your mother think is wrong with Charles?

Fanny: Oh, you know, people say that—

Mary: Charles has been known to drink. I know. Gossip is so cruel. You know the true things. When your mother is here she will see how decent my brother is.

Fanny: I know it's almost crazy. But I understand what makes Mother the way she is about people drinking.

(With difficulty)

If you'd known what my father was like. If you had seen him . . .

(She shudders)

There never was any money; not any. He took it all for drink. She'd hide me from him when he came home reeling and cursing. Somehow she managed to take care of me; to bring me up. God knows how she did it, but she did. She swore my life would never be like hers. Always she had hopes for me and belief in me. I know it's hard to make allowances—

Mary: Yes. It's hard to keep remembering what has made people the way they are.

Fanny: I owe my mother so much. I owe her everything. But— I love Charles.

Mary: Of course you do. We both do.

Fanny: Oh, Miss Mary, what shall I do?

Mary: My dear, you cannot imagine how flattering it is for me to have a young girl in love come to me for advice. But perhaps you're right to do it. Old maids were ever dauntless defenders of romance . . . brothers or no. Romance: there's always conspiracy in it. Well, then, we shall have a small conspiracy. You and my brother and I.

Fanny: Will that be romantic?

Mary: We'll ask your mother here. You'll see how agreeably we live here. She'll see that my brother isn't—what does she say—libidinous and wild and ruinous to those about him. Oh, Fanny, who knows better than you? Who could see my brother without loving him?

Fanny: I couldn't, Miss Mary. You know that.

Mary: (Whispering for the effect) Good, then! We are dark and devious conspirators. We will win, my dear. Gracious, how smug you must think me with my "we will win"! But you see, I am now decided that I shall be the only woman in the

world who could welcome a brother's wife and make a friend
of her.

(She kisses Fanny's forehead)

Go as thou must, my child, and God prosper thee.

Coleridge: (Enters from the door to the inner room, carrying a
sheet of paper in his hand. His stature and manner have
undergone considerable change. He moves easily now, free of
the bent and broken aspects of before. His spirits are free and
full and expansive) Mary, see what I have done! Charles,
Charles! Where is he?

Emma: (She has entered behind him, at his heels) Oh, it's a
poem! Mr. Coleridge has written a poem.

Coleridge: Only a fragment; but read!

Mary: (Sadly) Oh, Coleridge, Coleridge.

Charles: (He enters now) I have the honor to bring two immor-
tals together. Miss Fanny Kelly, Coleridge.

(Fanny curtsies)

Coleridge: (Pays no attention) Read!

Charles: This is *Miss Kelly*, Coleridge!

Coleridge: (Commanding) Read!

Charles: (From the sheet of paper he reads a verse) "Beneath
yon birch with silver bark,

And boughs so pendulous and fair,

The brook falls scatter'd down the rock;

And all is mossy there!"

Mary: (She holds both her hands to head) That was to be a
letter to your wife!

Charles: (Repeating fondly) "The brook falls scatter'd . . ."

(Shakes his head in hopeless admiration. Savoring the
word)

"Scatter'd."

(Continuing)

"And there upon the moss she sits,

The Dark Ladie in silent pain."

Coleridge: (Cutting in on Charles so that they read the next
simultaneously. Coleridge rather impatiently corrects
Charles' cadence)

"The heavy tear is in her eye."

(Charles drops the sheet of paper and looks expectantly to
Coleridge for the last line, as yet unwritten)

(Coleridge makes visible effort for the last time. Points his
finger at Charles, marking the rhythm, and murmurs the
last line again)

"The heavy tear is in her eye."

(Then in a strong triumphant voice he finishes it)

"And drops and swells again."

Fanny: Such lovely lines.

Charles: Archangel!

(His eyes go to the mantelpiece and he starts as he sees
that the vial of laudanum is missing. To Mary)

Mary, did you take it?

Mary: No, I believed him.

(Head gesture again)

Oh, now it all starts up again!

Charles: (Looking back at Coleridge, bitterly) A man with a
will of iron.

Mary: Coleridge. Coleridge. Coleridge.

Emma: (Exuberantly) Oh, Mr. Coleridge, would you inscribe
those lines in my album?

Coleridge: Why, of course, my dear.

(It's the first time he has really noticed her)

Why, Charles, who is this exquisite child?

Charles: (Walking away in disgust) Oh, I told you about her.

Coleridge: (He goes upstage towards the portrait of the child,
the lamb, and the roses hanging over the mantelpiece. Coleridge is high. Emma, frightened, still tags him with her
album)

Why, she is *that* child!

(Points to the portrait. He turns to Fanny, who recoils
slightly)

Look into her eloquent eyes. Listen to her pleading voice.
Her words are words of wisdom. Garner them up in thy
heart, when the evil days come, the days in which thou
shalt say, "I find no pleasure in them!" Remember her as thus
she stood . . .

Mary: Oh, Coleridge, do sit down.

Coleridge: (Impassioned. Direct to the portrait) Poor child, must thou, too, be reminded of the thorns that lurk beneath the flowers?

(Staring again at Emma. He speaks to Mary)

What an extraordinary resemblance, Mary! Did she sit for this portrait?

Mary: It was painted fifty years ago.

Charles: It reminds Mary of the happiest days of her life, when she was a lass in the country.

Mary: Maybe they were only the *second* happiest days. I've got a feeling; oh, you can tell about these feelings . . . The happiest ones are still to be, for us. For you and me and Fanny.

Emma: (Pestering Coleridge by tugging his sleeve) Mr. Coleridge, you said you'd inscribe your lines—

Mary: (Musing on) Our days to come—here, dwelling in happiness. Oh, Charles, don't you feel it, too?

Charles: When you say it, Mary. When you put it into words, then of course I feel it.

Emma: (With her album) You promised me those lines, Mr. Coleridge. You promised—

Coleridge: Have I ever broken a promise?

Charles: Oh, my God!

Mary: The man passes credibility!

Coleridge: Not only shall I inscribe this fragment to its finish, but I shall write you six more, eight more, twelve more— twenty. Paper! Quills! Ink! I need no other ingredients for immortality.

(Emma hurries to the writing table for paper)

Emma: O-o-o, in *my* book! And him so roaring famous!

(Returns to Coleridge with the paper)

Charles: (To Emma) Twenty poems, Emma. He promises twenty. Hurry, child, you may get half of one.

Mary: (Quietly) And still partake of immortality.

(Emma and Coleridge go off into dining room)

Mary: (To Fanny) Preposterous. Vulnerable. Comic. Pathetic. In short, irresistible. Our great ones. You'll learn how much they are our little children.

Fanny: (Laughing) Oh, Miss Lamb. And I was so in awe of the great. Now I've seen him, how could I ever be afraid again?

Charles: That tears it! My sister's had you while my back was turned.

(Sarcastic)

Now you see we geniuses are only people to be taken care of.

Mary: Fanny, Fanny, don't worry about taking care of other people. We'll all three be here together—please God!—and we'll take care of one another.

Fanny: Oh. Yes, of course, Miss Lamb . . . Mercy, I've stayed much too long. Whatever am I to say to Mother?

Mary: Say to your mother that my brother and I wish so much she will do us the happiness to come here to see us in our home.

Charles: Oh, you women! You two women! What in God's name will we do with her here?

Mary: We will show her, my dear, that we have neither horns nor tails.

Charles: But Mary, Mrs. Kelly is . . . is . . .

Mary: Charles, Charles, are you afraid of a woman?

Charles: Frankly, yes.

Fanny: Charles!

Charles: Not of you, my dear. Not quite, I mean . . . except when you go away from me.

Fanny: As I should have gone long ago. Good night, Miss Mary.

(Takes Mary's hand)

And thank you.

Mary: Good night, my dear. We understand, don't we? Conspirators, remember?

(Fanny and Charles exit stage left. Mary goes down to the writing table and stands over it looking at various manuscripts)

(Charles returns and comes down to writing table with her)

Mary: Oh, she's so lovely, Charles.

Charles: I trust we haven't wearied you too much.

Mary: Charles, no one is wearied by looking at loveliness.

(A slight pause)

I'm so unwearied and you're so happy. There's so much on earth for both of us.

(Indicating the manuscripts on the table)

Some of it's here, Charles.

Charles: Good. There's time before supper.

Mary: (As they sit down across from one another) Oh, it'll be heaven to crumple papers and splash ink, and swear at each other again!

 (They work silently for a moment. Mary raises her head slowly and looks a moment at Charles before she speaks) Charles?

Charles: Yes, Mary.

Mary: I think you know I'll try not to need you so much.

Charles: Yes, Mary, I know.

 (They work again)

Mary: Oh, the Devil! I do get so stuck in these comedies. I'm tired of all these young women dressed up as boys. I sometimes think Shakespeare lacked imagination.

Curtain

ACT TWO

Time: A Thursday night, one month later.
Scene: Same as in Act 1.

There is a buffet table located upstage center; lower stage left, a whist table surrounded by four chairs; lower stage right, another whist table with four chairs around it. The inner room, suggested in Act 1 by a door, is now lighted. The picture of the lamb, the roses, and the girl is missing from the center of the mantelpiece. Five new and larger Hogarths (oils) are hung on the back wall, while two additional ones are stacked near the fireplace. The set is brightly lit; the atmosphere is cheerful, intimate, and relaxed. As the curtain goes up we see Charles and Fanny on alone. Charles is nearly finished hanging the new Hogarths. Fanny is studying them.

Charles: I think "The Gaming House" here—
    (He indicates left of the fireplace)
and "The Tavern" there.
    (To the right of the fireplace)
Fanny: (She peers at "The Tavern" painting shyly) Oh!
Charles: What's the matter?
Fanny: I . . . I just saw what that woman's doing. And her stocking's all torn.
    (Turning away modestly)
Charles: (Chuckling) Hogarth's eye missed nothing. And see this charming lady spitting wine across the table at her friends.
Fanny: (Swallowing) It's fine you take pleasure in them.
Charles: I cannot keep away from them nor keep from thinking of the artist. Those lovely English faces!
    (He laughs again)
Every bruise, every pock mark, a masterpiece. The courage the man had and the impudence! Painting a portrait of some mighty lord one day, and the next reproduce his face on a visitor in a brothel scene! These wonders! These obscene realities! The whole history of the time caught on a gin shop sign: "Drunk for a penny, dead drunk for tuppence, clean straw for nothing!"
    (He laughs again)

Mary: (Entering with a tray. She whispers to Fanny) My dear,
our conspiracy is enlarged. Becky is our newest member. She
has actually allowed me her oven for these little jam tarts
which are calculated to melt any mother's heart.

(Puts down tray. Off to scullery)

Fanny: Oh, she thinks of everything. She is doing everything
for my mother's pleasure when she comes.

(She looks back at the Hogarths ruefully)

But Charles, Charles, I fear mother will not be able to grasp
Mr. Hogarth's realities.

Charles: I will not hide my Hogarths! Fanny, I will do anything else for your mother. I think we have already done
everything else. We've told those of our friends who might
be a bit too high-pitched for your mother that we should not
be at home tonight. Thursday nights! The night we always
had for our friends. But Hazlitt, for instance, is apt to be a
little over-confiding about his love life. We sent a note to his
lodgings. We could not—maybe we would not—bring ourselves to lie to Coleridge, but God grant that he will be
otherwise occupied.

Fanny: Mother and I have been such a nuisance. You've been
so kind. Your sister is so gracious. I'm so glad she likes me.
She does like me, doesn't she?

Charles: Of course, she does. She's been herself these past
weeks. She's well.

Fanny: You say "well" now. Was she ill? What was her illness?

Charles: My dear Fanny, I thought I could cheat it but I find I
cannot. My poor dear dearest sister has the sorest of all mal-
adies. She is sometimes beyond her mind.

Fanny: (Taking Charles' hand) I knew that, Charles. I've been
told.

Charles: I think you know not how deep it goes. This last time,
when I said she was away visiting friends, she wasn't. She
was—

Fanny: I know. I know, Charles.

Charles: You've seen her, Fanny. You've seen what she's like
here at home. But in that place—I tried to see her but it was
no use. I couldn't see her but, alas, I could hear her pouring
out the past, a medley between inspiration and possession.

Ah, Fanny, if you knew all about her you would have pity, and pity begets love, and love admiration.

Fanny: Dear Charles.

Charles: And it continues, Fanny. It goes on and on. Each time I have thought it was the last. Nine years I've hoped.

Fanny: Oh, God, what people are asked to endure.

Charles: I wanted to tell you before but I feared what it might do to us.

Fanny: Charles, do you think my love for you is such a poor weak thing that it will break under its share of this burden? For God's sakes, respect my love for you.

Charles: Fanny, you have understood all the time. God grant you go understanding forever.

Fanny: That's my part, Charles. Saint Charles.

(Fanny kisses Charles' hand)

But it will be all fine tonight. I feel it in my bones.

Charles: And you must trust those beautiful bones, my dear.

Fanny: They're not beautiful but let's trust them anyway.

(Noticing the figurines on the mantel)

Ah, who changed them around again?

(She changes them so that they are looking at each other)

They should be looking at each other, the poor darlings.

(She comes downstage to Charles)

You know for all Mother's protestations against the celebrated, I think she has a sneaking desire to meet them. I know she will be won over.

Charles: We'll all be at our best. The hearth is swept, the mutton's tender, and I am become a model Englishman. And when I win that bonus . . . When that frigate arrives for her cargo of tea, I shall truly be walking along velvet.

Fanny: You said the ship's name was "Favorite." Surely that's good luck.

Charles: (Bitterly) It will mean good luck to all East India House. A prize cargo; grog for the ship's crew, bonuses for the clerks, and another bloody million for our slave drivers.

Dyer: (George Dyer enters from stage left wing. He carries the usual complement of books. He wears a shawl fastened with a large safety pin, horse blanket dimension. He bows) I bid you good evening. I am back from my stroll.

Charles: Ah, the return of Ulysses. Congratulations on your firm stand against the sirens.

Fanny: (As Dyer fails to unfasten the pin) Mr. Dyer, do let me help you off with your shawl.

Dyer: Thank you, my dear young lady. It is most difficult for me to accustom myself to these fastenings and unfastenings. I fear I am but the slave of fashion.

(Fanny removes the shawl and goes stage right and sits near the whist table and begins sewing, her reticule being in the chair. Dyer goes up to inspect the new Hogarths)

Oh, excellent, sir. The series portraying "The Rake's Progress," is it not?

Charles: It is, and God knows I could no more resist buying it than I can afford paying for it.

Dyer: That's somewhat curious. I had been under the impression that there were eight pictures to the series. A trick of memory, no doubt.

Charles: No, there are eight. I told that idiot at the gallery not to send the eighth one but he sent it anyway. Now I must take the damned thing back again. I dare not risk the picture of Bedlam in this house.

Fanny: (Slowly) Charles, I have heard if those who are afraid of thunder storms will once face the lightning, they will be cured of their terrors. I've been thinking—if perhaps Miss Mary would see the picture . . . Have you ever thought of that?

Charles: I have, Fanny, but I have not yet the courage to put her to the test. No, the picture must go back.

Dyer: If I might be of service, sir, I am at your command. I will pass by the gallery within the hour and thus could spare you the journey.

Charles: Thank you, George.

Fanny: (She has been sewing with her back to the others and is suddenly vexed at her own sewing) Oh, the Devil!

(Mary enters, carrying her sewing in her hands)

Mary: Are you in trouble, my dear?

Fanny: I cannot set this whale bone straight.

Mary: (Going to her) Let me see, perhaps I can help.

(Mary takes the sewing from Fanny's hands, holds it up so that we see it is a corset)

Stand up a moment, my dear.

    (Fanny does so but she is timid with Charles being in the room. Mary fits the corset to Fanny and then illustrates how she must sew it)

Here, like this.

Fanny: Oh, thank you.

    (Sitting again)

I wish the wardrobe mistress at the theater had fewer thumbs. It's a pretty pass when an actress must mend her own—

    (Whispers)

stays.

Mary: Yes, Fanny.

    (She sits in a nearby chair)

Fanny: (Watching Mary sew, swiftly and efficiently. Discouraged, she drops her work in her lap) You're so skillful! I wish I had the gift.

Mary: It's no gift, my dear. When I was young I spent years apprenticed to a dressmaker.

    (Begins a meditation which continues in rhythm with her needle-work)

She was *my* India House . . . You see, school was for my brothers, not for me. But when I was very little I had the good fortune to tumble into a library . . . My grandmother was housekeeper at the country house of a gentleman of learning.

    (Charles overhears this soliloquy and begins an apprehensive approach behind Mary's chair—fearing the danger of Mary's memory)

Mary: I read all the dramas . . . all the histories . . . all the Bibles.

    (She is amused now and speaks as if she were half-kidding herself)

I think I was about nine when I was overwhelmed by the Koran and became a devout Mohammedan.

    (Laughing)

I used to wake in the night and weep because my grandmother was not a Believer and so, of course, she could never walk across the silken thread into Paradise but must fall off into Hell . . . There were statues in the library . . . I learned

Latin because I wanted to know what the inscriptions on
them said . . . I taught Charles his Latin from tombstones in
the churchyard near my grandmother's . . . He was such a
dear little boy—so quick—so filled with delight . . . He used
to bring me posies.

(Laughs softly)

I would have nothing but the bluebells with the red in them
and the *double* daffodils, and I remember telling him never
to gather me daisies, they were so common . . . What a
shocking young prig I must've been!

(Charles has shadowed this whole recollection with a
growing uneasiness, but at the finish of the last line he
sighs with relief and turns back to the paintings again)

Fanny: You make me ashamed of myself. You know everything
and I know nothing. I don't know history, I can barely do a
sum, I have not a single word of Latin!

Mary: (Bites off a thread, puts her sewing in a reticule, and
rises and goes to Fanny's chair) I think you have, my dear.
You already know the first Latin conjugation: "Amo, Amas,
Amat."

(Turning towards the scullery)

Now, I must see to Becky again; our anxiety for perfection
tonight ruffles her, poor thing.

(Mary exits through scullery)

Fanny: (At a knock on the door) If it's Mother, I just arrived.
Now remember, Charles.

Charles: (Going to her) A kiss for good luck.

(Kisses her quickly and goes to answer the door)

Mary: (From the scullery) Was that a knock?

Fanny: (Whispering) Yes, Charles has gone to the door.

Mary: (Whispering) It will be your mother?

Fanny: Yes, it must be.

(She holds up crossed fingers)

Mary: (Nodding and crossing her fingers) For luck. Oh, we're
going to have it.

Coleridge: (He enters as if pursued and then raises his hands
over his head in dramatic despair) Oh, Mary, Mary, help me!

(He sinks into a chair)

Mary: (She raises her hands to her temples) Oh, my God, this
happens.

Charles: Atlas! He has dropped the world from his shoulders and now drags it behind him.

Fanny: Oh, Charles, what shall we do?

Mary: (A calming gesture to Fanny) We've had this so often before.

(To Coleridge)

Coleridge, what is the matter now?

Coleridge: Matter? What is not the matter?

Charles: Coleridge, this is Miss Fanny Kelly.

(Fanny curtsies automatically. Coleridge pays no attention to her)

Mary: Well, tell us, Coleridge. What is it?

Coleridge: The hounds of hell draw closer. They snap at my heels.

Mary: Yes, my dear. I'm sure, I'm sure.

Charles: Oh, God, Southey must be come to London.

Coleridge: Come to London? The fiend has tracked me down even unto my wretched dwelling place. My traitorous land-lady—that venal bag who had sworn on the body of her bastard never *never* to reveal my whereabouts, then tells me Southey has come while I am away at my apothecary's. And he has left a message with her. He, the poet laureate of England, has left a message with this . . .

(He chokes in fury)

this . . . this . . .

(Almost a scream of desperation)

Oh, WHY is there no female equivalent of Judas!

Charles: He's upset.

Mary: Coleridge, my dear, could you tell us more clearly about the "fiends" and the "hounds" and the "venal bags"?

Coleridge: You know the message he left? He said that if I did not return to my abused wife and my fat child that he, Southey, would convey me, by force if necessary, back to my intolerable hearth. Oh, Mary, now of all times I seek sanctuary.

Mary: Oh, Coleridge, this is too unpretty. The laureate drag-ging the great poet . . . You see, tonight we want it all calm and pleasant here. Could you not seek refuge somewhere else?

Coleridge: Mary! A new betrayal.

(He drops his head hopelessly)

I bleed!

Mary: No one wants you to bleed, Coleridge. Stay here and heal your wounds, of course. But, you see, this night is a most delicate occasion for all of us and so you must be quiet, my dear. You must be calm.

Charles: Calm! Quiet! Oh, God, if he could just be invisible.

Mary: (Pacifying Charles) Charles, please.

(To Coleridge)

Coleridge, we are playing a game. I know we may not look it but we are, and if you must be here with us tonight you must play it, too.

Coleridge: Games? I'm not much good at games, Mary. But if you want me to, of course. Now what shall I do? Whom shall I play? What words do I say? Where is my station?

Mary: It's for Charles' sake. Fanny's mother is coming tonight. We are told she is a little apprehensive about people . . . well, people like us. We must show her on this, her first visit, that we are quiet and usual folk. So, Coleridge, just until we get acquainted with her would you wait inside?

Coleridge: I will vanish into thin air. The lady will never know I was born. I will go and stare at the wall and count my hands.

Mary: Oh, there is a better pastime for you than that. There has come for you a letter here. Addressed to you in our care.

(As if she were speaking to a child)

And do you know who it's from? It's from Wordsworth. Your giant, Wordsworth.

Coleridge: Where is it? I must have it at once.

Mary: It's in the inner room. On the small table by the divan. We've kept it there for you.

Charles: Yes, and for God's sakes lie on the divan and read it.

Mary: Charles, please. Come, Col,

(She leads him toward the door)

come in and read your letter. And after you've read it, lie on the divan a little while. You've had small rest of late, I know.

(Mary and Coleridge go off to inner room)

Fanny: Oh, Charles, how do I look? I think I've aged twenty years since Mr. Coleridge came in.

Charles: My dear, it's difficult to see your beauty through the smokes of Hell that our dear Coleridge has raised.

Fanny: Oh, God grant that Mother doesn't come quite yet. Mr. Coleridge is—please, Charles—he's a little upsetting.

Charles: Yes. Coleridge is a little upsetting. And Vesuvius erupts mother's milk.

(A knock on the door)

Fanny: Oh, let me kiss *you* for luck at this knock on the door.

(They kiss)

Charles: I wish all London would come a-knocking.

(He goes off to answer the door. He returns in a moment bringing Mrs. Kelly. Mrs. Kelly is a middle-aged woman, well dressed, perhaps over-dressed. She is a tense, suspicious woman who is jealous of her own importance; she is a stage mother in the extreme)

Fanny: (Going to her in a humble and obedient manner) I just came from the theater, Mother.

(Kisses her cheek)

Mrs. Kelly: Baby!

(To Charles)

They work my baby so hard!

(Mrs. Kelly sweeps the room with a critical eye and begins to move around it—chair to table to bookcase—in an inspection tour. Charles and Fanny are both on strict manners, a little anxious that Mrs. Kelly find everything pleasing. They follow her)

Charles: (Somewhat ill at ease, tries a pleasantry) That's the trouble with modern drama. It's so often all work and no play.

(As the joke goes flat)

That's a sort of pun, Ma'am.

Mrs. Kelly: Is it indeed?

(She pauses)

A more spacious room than I had thought.

Charles: Oh, it's a simple place but it's—loathsome.

(Unsuccessful laugh)

Fanny: Mother, aren't these fine old candlesticks?

(Indicating the table)

Mrs. Kelly: (Reluctant admiration) Hm!

Charles: A gift of a friend, brought from Germany.

Mrs. Kelly: Foreign. Bless me, so many candles, and tallow so cruel dear now.

Fanny: See the curtains, Mother, Miss Mary made them herself.

Mrs. Kelly: (Fingering them) Most tasteful.

Fanny: And all the books, did you ever see so many? The wonderful old folios and the new books by all the great modern writers . . . and all inscribed. Oh, Mr. Wordsworth and Mr. Southey and Mr. Coleridge and—oh, all of them—they wouldn't dream of having anything published until Mr. Lamb approved of it.

Charles: Oh, Miss Kelly—

Mrs. Kelly: (Running her finger against the books to find dust. She snaps some from her fingertips) Most gratifying, I'm sure.

   (Noticing Dyer and the many books scattered about his chair on the floor)

And all these books? What's he doing with all these books?

Charles: He's reading them, Ma'am. Odd way to treat books, isn't it?

   (He forces a laugh and Fanny shakes her head at him nervously)

George.

   (A little more distinctly)

George. This is Mrs. Kelly.

Dyer: (Rising. He drops a book) I bid you good evening, Madam.

Mrs. Kelly: (As Fanny stoops to recover the book) Oh, don't touch it, Baby. So dusty . . .

   (Mary enters the room quietly from the inner room. She is self-possessed, at the height of her grace and dignity as the cordial mistress of her home)

Charles: Mrs. Kelly, this is my sister, Mary.

Mary: Good evening, Mrs. Kelly, you are most welcome.

Mrs. Kelly: (Surprised at Mary's poise) I have heard a great deal about Miss Lamb.

   (Overly solicitous)

How are you feeling, my dear?

Mary: Very well, thank you.

Mrs. Kelly: I am overwhelmed to be here on a Thursday night. One hears so much of the Lambs' Thursday nights.

Mary: This will be a most quiet one, Mrs. Kelly. So many of our friends must be away.

Mrs. Kelly: One hears such curious tales of their ways of living.

Mary: I'm sure one does. But one does not always hear the truth.

Mrs. Kelly: But this—
  (Indicating the room in a sweeping gesture)
  this could be the home of any quiet, conventional English family.

Mary: (Pleased) You could not have paid it a higher compliment, Mrs. Kelly. That is what we so wanted it to be, and for us who live in it to be—quiet and conventional, too. Do sit down, Mrs. Kelly. Will you take tea?

Mrs. Kelly: (Fanny goes to the buffet and prepares to help Mary) Bless me, tea! There's not many that can afford it these days, it's so wicked dear.

Mary: Thank you, Fanny. Will you take this to your mother?

Charles: I'd forgotten how refreshing a cup of tea may be.

Mrs. Kelly: You find it so? I should think it would be thin stuff for a connoisseur of brandy. Or is it gin?

Mary: Oh, both. My brother and I find them best combined in a large tankard heavily laced with hot, black rum.

Mrs. Kelly: Bless me!

Fanny: (Choking a little) Oh, Miss Lamb is teasing, Mother.

Mrs. Kelly: So I trust. It would seem strange that her apothecary would allow her to drink spirits. A half pound of tea costs a pretty penny.

Charles: A pretty penny and a handsome sum. Why is money always described in terms of beauty?

Mrs. Kelly: The worst thing for England, a tea famine. Mr. Lamb, you're in public office; can you explain what causes this?

Charles: It's due to the greed of East India House that there's no tea in England today. They won't pay the poor devils who man their fleets, and so there *are* mutinies and scuttlings.

The tea rots in India until the people here will pay any price for it. When they'll pay forty times its value—and Mr. Wilberforce times it precisely—then India House brings in a cargo . . . Brings it in by tossing a few bonuses.

Mrs. Kelly: Tossing bonuses? Do you stand to catch one, sir?

Fanny: Yes, he does, Mother!

Mrs. Kelly: Why do you keep things from me, Baby? It hurts Mother.

Charles: When the frigate "Favorite" docks, all London will hear of my good fortune. I plan on running from door to door spreading the news.

Mary: (She has been busy with her duties as hostess. Her eyes move around the room. Now she notices the mantelpiece and she notices that the figurines of the shepherd and the shepherdess have been moved again. She goes to the mantelpiece and speaks almost angrily) Who does this? Who keeps doing this?

   (The figurines are changed back to their old order. To Charles, sarcastically)

Mice, I suppose.

   (Guilty looks are exchanged between Charles and Fanny)

Dyer: (In trouble with his book) Drat! Drat! Drat! Oh, I beg your pardon.

Charles: Good God, George, what monstrous catastrophe is this?

Dyer: The pages are uncut. Perhaps the old books are best . . .

Charles: (Picks up a letter opener from the whist table adjacent and hands it to Dyer) Here, try this letter opener.

Dyer: Thank you, sir.

   (He bungles the operation)

Thank you, sir. The author, I fear, has been at some disadvantage. I've been enabled to read only every fourth page.

Charles: (Taking the book away from him, cuts the pages, and hands it back to Dyer) Permit me.

   (He drops the letter opener on the table again)

Emma: (She enters from dining room excitedly. Coleridge's agitated figure can be seen behind her. To Mary) He started to write but he's broken all the quills and he is much upset.

Coleridge: (Calling from within) Mary! Pst! Pst!

Charles: Splendid! He was to lie down and rest.

Mary: (To Mrs. Kelly) This is Emma. Emma Isola, Mrs. Kelly. Have you finished your lesson, child?

    (Mary begins moving toward the writing table to get more paper for Coleridge)

Emma: Yes, Aunt Mary.

    (To Mrs. Kelly)

Aunt Mary is teaching me French.

Mary: It's a recreation for both of us.

Mrs. Kelly: Are you not afraid of the effect of the French language on the pure young English mind?

Mary: I am more afraid of the effect of the French language on the pure young English accent.

    (She moves upstage now, the paper and quills in her hand)

Forgive me a moment.

    (She goes)

Mrs. Kelly: I find anything French most foreign—especially the people.

Charles: I have friends who have traveled much in France. They tell me the people are French wherever you go. What an overwhelming effect that must have!

Mrs. Kelly: (To Emma, all sugar) Sit down, my child. You live here?

Emma: Yes, I've been here a month now.

Mrs. Kelly: You like it?

Emma: Oh, very much.

Mrs. Kelly: I suppose you're kept busy helping Miss Lamb?

Emma: Oh, no, Becky does the work.

Mrs. Kelly: Becky?

Emma: The housekeeper.

Mrs. Kelly: Oh, they keep a servant? Yes, I suppose they have to with a sick woman in the house.

    (To Fanny)

Although, I must say, my dear, that if I hadn't heard so many tales about the poor thing I would have thought her no different from anyone else.

Fanny: She is no different, only more patient.

Mrs. Kelly: (Back to Emma) I suppose you've learned to be
good and keep quiet while Mr. Lamb works at his writings.

Emma: He's never told me to, Ma'am.

Mrs. Kelly: Tell me, child, does he work every night?

Emma: When he's not too tired. He says when the pension
comes he will write every night and day.

Mrs. Kelly: He expects a pension? Does he say when?

Emma: (Calmly quoting) When those damned slave drivers
have their first Christian emotion.

Mrs. Kelly: What?

Emma: (Giggling in a naughty indulgence) He says that it will
be the day after Hell freezes over.

Mrs. Kelly: (Almost admonishing Fanny) You see, you hear
the child's language. That's what comes of being thrown in
with a band of literary characters.

(To Emma again)

It's a great privilege for you to meet the famous people who
come here.

Emma: I never can get anybody to inscribe in my album.

(Mary re-enters)

Charles: How is he?

Mary: Wordsworth wrote him an unfortunate letter. But I
quieted him, I think.

Dyer: Oh, drat it!

(He has cursed and so he immediately apologizes)

I ask your pardon. I was pressed into employing strong
language.

Mary: Oh, George, let me help you!

(Dyer extends the book again and the letter opener is used
by Mary to split some more pages for him)

Mrs. Kelly: Tell me, what is it like when they are here? Is there
much carousing? Do they drink much?

(Mary turns defensively)

Fanny: Oh, Mother, please . . .

Becky: (Entering from the scullery) Miss, how many times do I
have to tell you to fill the cold water jugs?

Emma: Oh, I'm sorry, Becky.

(Off to the scullery)

Becky: (Muttering) Nothing done and them asking high-flown strangers in to give a body more work.

(Off to the scullery)

Mrs. Kelly: Bless me, what a way for a servant to talk.

Mary: (She has finished cutting pages for George Dyer, and at Mrs. Kelly's remark she turns toward her, with the book and the letter opener still in her hand) You must forgive our Becky as we do. Her poor old father's mind left him, and she is in dreadful anxiety to afford a quiet place where he may have proper care.

Mrs. Kelly: What a waste of worry and money when there's public places for him and his kind. She ought to pack him off to Bedlam—

Fanny: Mother!

Mrs. Kelly: Well, that's what Bedlam's for, isn't it?—To put the lunatics in—

Charles: Oh, Mrs. Kelly—

Mrs. Kelly: Oh! Oh, I beg your pardon. I only meant poor man—and poor Becky too!

Mary: (She calmly hands the book back to Dyer but retains the letter opener in her hand. Directly to Mrs. Kelly) You must not feel too sorry for either of them, Mrs. Kelly.

Charles: (Trying to break the tension) Shall we have a hand of whist, Ma'am? The cards are there.

Mary: (Restraining Charles with a gesture) Just a moment, Charles, there's no need to change the subject. Mrs. Kelly must understand this.

(The key of her voice is low at first but soon reveals a passion)

The insane in their fancies do not suffer as the sane do under *real* evil; under poverty, or the loss of friends, or the knowledge of having done wrong. Only they *must* have tenderness. You do not realize how susceptible they are. A hired nurse may have skill and conscience, but if she is not tender there is nothing—nothing but suffering.

(Moving toward Mrs. Kelly)

They cannot ask tenderness, but if they are denied it they must live in eternal despondency.

(Excited)

When you talk of packing them off to the city madhouse you talk of slow murder. You talk of filth and nakedness, whips and chains, starvation save for a bucket of slops. And, worst of all, you talk of the horrible, the obscene mockery of the public.

(Charles is rooted in fear as the room crystalizes. Mary is now impassioned, and she gestures with her right hand which still holds the letter opener)

Good God Almighty! They make a show of them—they come and laugh at them—And you—you—you say—

Charles: Mary, for God's sakes!

(She brings her arm down slowly and as she does she notices, as if for the first time, that she holds the letter opener in her hand as if it were a weapon. With a shudder of realization, she opens her hand and drops it to the floor, and Charles comes downstage to pick it up. Mary wipes her hands on her dress)

Mary: All thick and wet and red. Oh, Charles, I have done this terrible thing!

Charles: Mary, don't—

Mary: (His voice restores her. She turns back, downstage, and there is a great change. Her face is serene) It's all right, Charles.

(She goes to the buffet and joins Emma. Mary pours tea, arranges a tray, and with her old sweet calm tones comes downstage to Mrs. Kelly at the whist table)

Mrs. Kelly must try a sweet. One of our special jam tarts.

(There is a knock on the door. Emma goes off to answer it)

Charles: Thank Heavens, it cannot be one of our nocturnal guests—or "knock-eternal" guests.

(There is the usual lack of appreciation of the pun)

I warn you, I'll repeat that pun till somebody laughs at it!

Mary: Tomorrow and tomorrow and tomorrow . . .

Emma: (Returning from the door first) I left the door open, I thought it might stop Uncle Charles' pun.

(Off to the scullery)

Charles: Hazlitt! You did not get our message?

Hazlitt: (Hazlitt is a dark-haired, well-built young man. He has fine eyes, an intelligent and sensitive face. You have the feeling that, now in his early thirties, he has been spared a great many of the hardships of life) I've not been back to my lodgings. What message?

Charles: No matter. We thought we would not be at home tonight.

Mary: Charles, please. Never mind about messages, Hazlitt. We're always at home to our friends.

Charles: Yes, we are here.

   (Half-heartedly)

Hazlitt, are you . . . are you all right?

Hazlitt: I shall never be all right again.

Charles: Oh, God!

Mary: My dear Hazlitt, Mrs. Kelly, Miss Kelly—Mr. Hazlitt.

Mrs. Kelly: Mr. *William* Hazlitt?

Hazlitt: Are there others?

Mrs. Kelly: I hope I see you well, sir.

Hazlitt: (Short, bitter laugh) I am a whited sepulchre containing the rotted corpse of a heart.

Charles: Things are as usual; we are to be spared nothing.

Hazlitt: I have been made the victim of the most outrageous cruelty.

Mrs. Kelly: Why, whatever's happened to you?

Hazlitt: I've been abandoned.

Charles: Another time Hazlitt, another time.

Mary: (She raises both her hands to her head again) Yes, Hazlitt, yes.

Hazlitt: After I endured the hardships of a journey to Scotland. After I abased myself before the divorce attorneys—

   (Breaking off as if the tale were too painful to recall)

Mrs. Kelly: (Shocked) He's a divorced man! Why, we're in the same room with a divorced man!

Fanny: Oh, Mother, he's a genius; he's a writer and a painter.

Mrs. Kelly: He's a divorced man! That's the kind of friends they have.

Charles: (Forcing laughter for Mrs. Kelly's benefit) That Hazlitt, what a tease!

Hazlitt: After my Spartan demeanor while my wife's frenzied pleading not to cast her off gnawed at my vitals, then to find that the woman who had sworn to be true had deserted me. Gone off, Ma'am, and with a commercial traveler.

(To Mrs. Kelly)

And you hope you see me well! How the Devil could you see me well?

Mary: Oh, come, come, Hazlitt. Have a drink!

Hazlitt: (Pained) Mary, do not try to console me, it is a hopeless thing—even for you. I am a broken man!

Charles: (Sharply) Do not worry her, Hazlitt!

(To Mrs. Kelly)

Don't mind him, Ma'am.

Mary: Charles, no matter what happens we must not apologize to our new friends for our old ones.

(Turning again to Hazlitt)

I'm sorry but I insist you look well.

(To the Kellys)

He is most ornamental as a Thursday man, but a more useful one on common days, when he drops in after a quarrel or a fit of the glooms.

Hazlitt: When I am in that condition—that usual condition with me—what is my possible use?

Mary: Our friends compliment us when they come to us for comfort.

Hazlitt: Mary, you are the most reasonable woman I know.

Mary: Sometimes.

Charles: Tell me, Hazlitt, what have you been doing?

Hazlitt: Oh, essays, lectures—what is there for me but work?

Mary: There are worse fates.

Hazlitt: Where is Coleridge?

Mary: I'm afraid he is—as usual.

Hazlitt: Does he continue his lectures at Cambridge?

Mary: We hear they've been well attended.

Charles: But the last two lectures the lecturer himself did not attend. 'Tis said he's gone sick upon them. He ain't well, that's certain.

Hazlitt: I not only don't pity sick people, I hate them!

Mrs. Kelly: This man's a brute! Poor Mr. Coleridge.

Mary: (Rather sharply) I can't bear that "poor."

Charles: She means she can't bear to hear such a man pitied.

Mary: I had rather not have you explain what I mean, Charles.

Mrs. Kelly: (Noticing the friction between Charles and Mary) Well, bless me!

    (Coleridge rushes in, suffering beneath a new burden of agony. He goes on his knees before Mary, holding a letter in his hand)

Coleridge: Mary! Mary!

Mary: Oh, Col, you promised us. You promised us! Oh, what now?

Coleridge: I've been thinking. I've been brooding. This letter—

Charles: Oh, this is my night. If once, just once, someone would enter that door without bleating.

Mary: Now what is it you've been brooding over?

Coleridge: Wordsworth has here

    (He indicates the letter)

insulted me.

Mary: Well, that may not be so mighty. Always you mistake the squall for the tempest.

Mrs. Kelly: (Who has been regarding Coleridge in horror. To Fanny) Who is this maniac?

Fanny: (Hushed tone) Mother! It's Mr. Coleridge.

Mrs. Kelly: That—is Coleridge?

Coleridge: I am the most ill-understood and ill-requited of all those who walk this earth.

Charles: Oh, good God, how ill-used can you become.

Mary: (Soothing Charles) Charles, no.

    (To Coleridge)

Col, what has he written that has so overset you?

Coleridge: Wordsworth here has called me a nuisance.

Charles: Why, the rascally old Lake Poet.

Coleridge: I, who have dwelt with him in his house. Walked with him beneath the sunsets, above the daffodils, beside the lakes.

Charles: Since when has Wordsworth quit walking *on* the lakes?

    (Hazlitt laughs)

Mary: I know. I know. Now try to calm yourself.

Coleridge: I—a nuisance? I've been on admirable behavior. Why, I've cut my laudanum to two quarts a week.

Mrs. Kelly: Jesus, Mary, and Joseph!

Charles: (False laughter for Mrs. Kelly) That Coleridge. So full of his own fun.

Coleridge: And Wordsworth cries, "Nuisance." *Nuisance!*

Charles: Oh, forget it, Coleridge. Stop worrying Mary.

Mary: Charles, please do not worry yourself over what might worry me.

Charles: I see no reason why you should squander your patience and strength on these imagined miseries.

Mary: (With a glance toward Fanny) You think I should save my fortitude for the real catastrophe? Perhaps you are right, my dear.

Mrs. Kelly: (To Fanny) You'd think they'd have enough sense to leave the poor thing alone.

Fanny: Mother, you see how strong she is. How they all depend on her.

Charles: (To Mrs. Kelly) Such a small woman, but a prop for the giants.

Mary: Come, Coleridge, you have not yet met Fanny's mother. Mrs. Kelly, Mr. Coleridge.

Mrs. Kelly: (Sniffing) I hope I see you well, sir.

Coleridge: (Recovering from a deep bow) You have a pretty sense of irony, Madam.

>   (Charles takes Coleridge by the arm and moves him upstage right toward the table. Mrs. Kelly moves toward the Hogarths. As she comes closer to them, she gasps. Hazlitt turns to her questioningly)

Hazlitt: Aren't they excellent? "The Rake's Progress." He's got them all but one. Charles, where's the scene in—

Coleridge: Hazlitt, for Heaven's sakes!

>   (With an indication toward Mary)

Hazlitt: Oh, of course.

Mrs. Kelly: And a young child living in the house with these things?

Hazlitt: You do not approve?

Mrs. Kelly: How can people hang such filthy pictures on their walls? I think they're disgusting.

Hazlitt: I think you have the distinction of being the first

Thursday night guest to find Hogarth so. You are a new
friend of the Lambs?

Mrs. Kelly: It's my first visit.

   (Sarcastic)

Most interesting to see the famous guests.

Hazlitt: Ah yes, as one visits a zoo. I urge you take a long look
at your host. He is lately become as famous as any man in
England.

Mrs. Kelly: Charles Lamb, famous? And what has he done?

   (Coleridge is uneasy and moves to interrupt and change
   the subject)

Hazlitt: Certainly you've read "Confessions."

Coleridge: Yes, Hazlitt.

   (To Mrs. Kelly)

Perhaps, then, Madam, your taste runs to landscapes? Something with a tree and a cloud? Maybe even going to the
length of a brook?

   (Savagely to Hazlitt)

Yes, it is best to cling to calmer subjects.

Mary: What did you say, Hazlitt? Confessions again? Who's
been confessing what now?

   (Charles grows uneasy)

Hazlitt: Haven't you read what's said of them?

Coleridge: Mary, Mrs. Kelly tells me she is passionately fond of
landscapes. I am about to suggest to her that we leaf through
some of these folios in search of pastoral delights.

Mrs. Kelly: I said no such thing about landscapes. What's all
this about Mr. Lamb's fame, Mr. Hazlitt?

Coleridge: (In a desperate last try) Now the landscape is to me
somewhat too placid. But, of course—

Fanny: What who said, Mr. Hazlitt?

Hazlitt: All England. The *London Journal* called the piece pain-
fully eloquent. The *Chronicle* said it was a terror-striking
composition. The *Philanthropist* prophesied that it would do
vast good.

   (To Charles)

It took enormous courage to do what you have done,
Charles.

Mary: (To Hazlitt) What did he do?
   (To Charles)
   Charles?
Mrs. Kelly: Baby, there's something else you haven't told
   Mother.
Fanny: But I know nothing about it.
Charles: I did nothing! I didn't do it. I didn't do it. I didn't
   do it!
Coleridge: He says he didn't write it. Don't you hear him? He
   says he didn't write it.
Hazlitt: What do you mean you didn't write it? Here it is,
   signed "Elia."
Charles: Oh, I wrote it but it was a joke, for God's sakes, and a
   very poor one.
Hazlitt: What is this, Charles, morbid modesty?
Mary: What's it about, Charles? Confessions of whom?
Charles: Well, of nobody. A fabulous character. It was a joke
   on an editor who turned out to be humorless. And, so, God
   help me, did Hazlitt.
   (He turns a withering glance on Hazlitt)
Mrs. Kelly: I would very much like to read it.
Charles: I beg your pardon, Mrs. Kelly, but I couldn't have you
   waste your time.
Coleridge: (Taking the magazine from Hazlitt) There's been
   enough talk about it. Here. Here's an end to it.
   (He stuffs it in his pocket, where it protrudes and Mrs.
   Kelly marks it well with a curious stare. Charles upstage
   to the table. Mary again speaks calmly and cordially to
   Mrs. Kelly)
Mary: Suppose we ladies have a hand of whist?
Emma: (As they move downstage right to whist table) I know
   how to play. I know how to play. I know how to play.
   (The ladies sit and the deal begins)
Hazlitt: (With Coleridge, he moves a little offstage left so that
   they may speak privately) Have you observed the strange be-
   havior of our host this evening? Have you noticed how he
   anoints with butter the mother of the fair one? How well I
   know the sad progression. First you meet the adored one.
   Oh, ecstasy! Then you meet the mother. Oh, horror! Then

you meet at the altar. Oh, disaster!

Coleridge: (In agreement with Hazlitt on Charles' situation, he shakes his head dolefully) Gone. Gone. Gone.

Charles: (Comes downstage to them with glasses of brandy) Will you drink, Coleridge?

Coleridge: I must. I must have something. I made a most foolhardy bargain with my apothecary. We agreed that I must reduce my ration by half, and the damned brute has kept his word.

(Fanny overhears and reacts)

Mrs. Kelly: Baby, mind your cards. Such talk.

Hazlitt: (To Coleridge) You should have a talk with De Quincey. I'm told he plans compiling a directory of London's apothecaries. Addresses, quantities, qualities, prices.

Coleridge: Really so? You soothe me.

Charles: England, my England. Half a guinea for half a pound of tea; a shilling for a hatful of opium.

Coleridge: De Quincey? Is he new to London?

Charles: Yes, new in London but old in the world. He had a note to me and then called at East India House. In ten minutes, I found that he has devoured half of the books in the universe.

Hazlitt: And half the opium.

Coleridge: What sort of fellow is he?

Hazlitt: What sort do you expect? One who spat on his benefactors and ran away from them. One who sleeps in ditches and gets up and shakes himself and takes his morning opium as other men take their porridge.

Coleridge: (To Charles) Oh. I cannot suppose you've invited him here?

Charles: (A stricken look at Mrs. Kelly) Oh, no! . . . Absolutely no!

Dyer: (Regretfully finishing the last page of his book, takes off his spectacles, rises, and steps out of the stockade of books around him on the floor) I fear I must bid the company good evening.

Mary: (Rising from whist table) Oh, I'm sorry, George.

Dyer: I have promised to attend a discussion of vital significance.

Charles: (A caricature of profundity) Ah? And what is to be discussed?

Dyer: The relative merits of Menander and Plotinus.

Charles: The world will be afire with it. You must not delay another instant!

Dyer: (Stoops and picks up several books) I must take with me the works of Menander, the poet. I've elected myself his advocate.

Hazlitt: Menander and Plotinus! George Dyer is a man of many projects. The last I heard of him he was to give us his autobiography. Has he written it yet, Mary?

Mary: (Sadly assents) But then he lost the manuscript.
 (To George)
 I hope you do not have far to go, George. I worry so when you're out of sight.

Dyer: It is not a distant walk; I need go only to Chiselhurst.

Mary: (Dismayed) It's half across London.
 (She sits)

Charles: George, you forget you were to do me a service as you passed the galleries.
 (Charles goes off through the door to the inner room)

Dyer: Ah, of course, of course. I fear my memory is not what it used to be. Only the other day on a walking excursion in the country I followed a path I remembered distinctly as leading straight to a quiet glade. Imagine my shock then when I later discovered it made a sharp turning to the right.

Mary: Shock, George?

Dyer: For I pursued the straight course and found myself in a small but rushing river.

Charles: (Returning with the Bedlam canvas, briskly hands it to George) You know the address.

Hazlitt: What is that, a picture that doesn't please you?
 (Mary looks up)

Charles: Yes. Go on, George. Good night.

Hazlitt (Turning the picture so that he may see it) What? You're sending back a Hogarth?

Coleridge: (Again interfering for Mary's sake) Hazlitt, no!

Charles: (Urging Dyer) Thank you, George. Good night.

(Dyer goes off left)

Mrs. Kelly: Bless me, walking into a river at his age. And your brother trusts him to deliver a picture, possibly valuable. Are they considered of value?

Mary: Another rubber of whist, Mrs. Kelly? You're so comfortably ahead you must let us try our revenge.

(Mary, Fanny, Emma, and Mrs. Kelly are seated)

Charles: Come, Hazlitt, try a *double* draft of brandy. Let's, for God's sakes, find something that will knock you speechless.

(The room is quieted. Thomas De Quincey sidles in, looks around as if he were entering a cathedral. He notices, particularly, the Hogarths. He is nineteen. His blond, emaciated appearance reflects a life of bitter poverty. Your eye is held by the erosion of hunger and narcomania, yet there is a sensitivity about the boy which makes him luminous)

Mrs. Kelly: (Shocked at De Quincey's bedraggled appearance) Bless me, what's this? Is the lad come begging pennies?

Mary: (Going to him) What is it you want, my boy?

Charles: (Turning from Coleridge and Hazlitt, thunderstruck) Oh, God! How all occasions do inform against me.

De Quincey: (Reverently to Charles) Good evening, sir.

Charles: My sister, Mary. This is Thomas De Quincey. I've told you about him.

Mary: But you never told me that—why, you're just a boy!

De Quincey: I'm nineteen, Ma'am.

(Gazing about the room)

Oh, Ma'am, I come here with my heart on its knees.

Charles: My God! Hazlitt, you know De Quincey.

Emma: He isn't famous, is he, Uncle Charles?

Charles: And Emma Isola, Mr. De Quincey. And yonder, the Kellys. Miss Fanny and her mother.

Mrs. Kelly: (Her handkerchief to her nostrils) Probably has some contagious disease.

Mary: (Hurries De Quincey to the buffet) Here, dear lad, have something to eat.

Charles: (To Coleridge) Coleridge, this is Thomas De Quincey, my old admirer.

De Quincey: (Awed, he puts down the plate) Coleridge!

(Charles hands back the plate to De Quincey and passes a nervous glance at Coleridge who, of course, is delighted that De Quincey has come)

De Quincey: Mr. Lamb . . .

(Mouthfuls)

I hope I haven't interrupted your conversation.

Charles: (Making the best of it) No, no, no, not at all. Emma, fetch Mr. Coleridge something to eat.

De Quincey: It would be so great a privilege for me to hear. Were you perhaps talking about poets? I mean the other poets?

Charles: (Making up for his nervousness at Coleridge and De Quincey being together by being over-genial) No, but we will if you want. Hazlitt, come talk about poets. Now, whom would you like?

De Quincey: Milord Byron?

Charles: Ah, yes. He is so great, in so little a way.

(To Mary)

Mary, don't you hate Byron?

Mary: Yes, Charles, I hate Byron.

Charles: That's right.

(To De Quincey)

Anyone else?

De Quincey: (Shocked but not yet distracted from his plate) Well, Mr. . . . Mr. Shelley?

Charles: Of Shelley, I think even Mr. Hazlitt would agree, his voice is worse than Southey, whose voice is the worst part about him except his laureateship.

De Quincey: (Putting down his plate, aghast) Good Heavens, Mr. Lamb!

Mary: Charles, leave the lad his heroes.

Coleridge: (Vulture-like) I've been led to understand from Mr. Hazlitt, young man, that you seek to enter the noble fields of literature.

De Quincey: Yes, sir.

Coleridge: And what glorious path will you pursue? The antiquuities, poetry, the drama, philosophy, or will you serve at the altar of a daintier muse?

De Quincey: I am mainly interested in murder, sir. I shall treat
it as I see it, as one of the fine arts.

Charles: (Forgetting himself and Mrs. Kelly's gasp. Fanny reacts, looks at Mary) What a charming young man! You must
come often.

   (To Coleridge)

Coleridge, more spirits?

Coleridge: No. I've renounced them.

   (To De Quincey)

And I thought I had renounced the other, but my hour has
not yet struck.

De Quincey: Nor has mine, sir, and I wonder if I wish to hear
it strike.

Coleridge: Then you keep the merciful murderer of pain always about you?

De Quincey: Oh, yes, sir. I have chosen between it and food.

Coleridge: Let us go in where we may be quiet. Young man, we
have things in common beyond poetry, beyond philosophy,
beyond the preoccupations of the usual man. Come—

   (He starts to move off with De Quincey)

Mrs. Kelly: (Rising and speaking to Mary) You permit this
poor young waif to fall into the clutches of that monster?

Coleridge: (To Mrs. Kelly) Madam, I advise you to hold your
tongue about matters which you cannot comprehend,
though this will, of course, condemn you to a lifetime of
silence.

   (Coleridge and De Quincey go into inner room)

Mrs. Kelly: (Angrily) Madam, you heard? I have been told
many scandalous tales about your Thursday night guests,
but when it comes to being insulted by a laudanum fiend—

Fanny: Mother, please . . .

Charles: Mrs. Kelly, please try to understand.

Mary: Yes, do try, Mrs. Kelly. I know, I know Coleridge is
oddly behaved. I know he's difficult. I know he seems at
times quite impossible, but he is a man who suffers much.
He lives in a world of his own terrors. We all have terrors, I
know, but not a whole world of them. Men like Coleridge, if
there are any others, give so much of beauty and truth that

their ways, their eccentricities, are all out-balanced by their immortal gifts. Please, please think of what he can do and not just of his occasional childish conduct, and you will not only forgive him but revere him. Please, Mrs. Kelly.

Mrs. Kelly: (Sitting again; pacified momentarily) W-e-l-l, geniuses, I suppose.

Becky: Miss Lamb?

Mary: Yes, Becky.

Becky: I've finished the punch, Ma'am.

Mary: Good, let's go in and start it. There's some hot food inside, or there should be if Becky's been faithful to her vows.

(She invites the company with a gesture)

Mrs. Kelly?

Mrs. Kelly: I must say that you do things handsomely.

Coleridge: (Re-entering with De Quincey. Coleridge has taken laudanum from De Quincey with the usual calming and liberating effect) And why do you seek the drug?

De Quincey: The cold and the darkness and the gray rats.

Mrs. Kelly: Poor child. No mother, I suppose.

Coleridge: I see. And the drug brings you riches; sleep and dreams.

De Quincey: Sometimes I lose the dreams.

Coleridge: More and more I keep them.

(Into a verse. As a music cue. As much verse as warranted)

> In Xanadu did Kubla Khan
> A stately pleasure-dome decree;
> Where Alph, the sacred river, ran
> Through caverns measureless to man
> Down to a sunless sea.
> So twice five miles of fertile ground
> With walls and towers were girdled round;
> And there were gardens bright with sinuous rills,
> Where blossomed many an incense-bearing tree;
> And here were forests ancient as the hills,
> Enfolding sunny spots of greenery.
> But oh! that deep romantic chasm which slanted
> Down the green hill athwart a cedarn cover!

A savage place! as old and as enchanted
As e'er beneath a waning moon was haunted
By woman wailing for her demon-lover!
And from this chasm, with ceaseless turmoil seething
As if this earth in thick fast pants were breathing,
A mighty fountain momently was forced
Amid whose swift half-intermitted burst
Huge fragments vaulted like rebounding hail,
Or chaffy grain beneath the thresher's flail;
And 'mid these dancing rocks at once and ever
It flung up momently the sacred river.
Five miles meandering with a mazy motion
Through wood and dale the sacred river ran,
Then reached the caverns measureless to man,
And sank in tumult to a lifeless ocean;
And 'midst this tumult Kubla heard from far
Ancestral voices prophesying war!

Fanny: (Enraptured, she rises) How did you know that wonderful place? Where did you see it?

De Quincey: (Knowingly) Probably in some wretched cottage
on an empty moor.

(Coleridge looks at De Quincey and smiles warmly, as if to
say, "Exactly!")

Has there ever been such poetry?

Mrs. Kelly: Bless me, is that the end?

De Quincey: No. Such dreams do not end.

Mrs. Kelly: Well, I'm sure it's very handsome poetry, although
what we've heard does sound most unnatural.

Mary: (To Coleridge) And you care what Wordsworth calls
you! Come in, Mrs. Kelly.

(Emma and Mary go off. Mrs. Kelly and Fanny hesitate)

Coleridge: (Expectantly) Well, Hazlitt?

Hazlitt: It's no "Ancient Mariner."

Charles: Coleridge, here's an observation: "Never tell your
dreams." Your poem is an owl that won't bear daylight.

Coleridge: (Scourged) And to this man I wrote a poem. A
poem to "gentlehearted Charles."

Charles: (The strain of the evening beginning to show) For

God's sakes, don't make me ridiculous anymore by terming
me "gentlehearted" in print.

> (Quoting derisively)

"Gentlehearted Charles, victim of sorrow and pain and
strange calamity." Gentle! Gentle, at best, means poor-
spirited. Call me fool, sinner, wastrel, drunkard—well, call
me any epithet which properly belongs to me, but not
gentle.

> (He goes up to Coleridge and puts his hand on his shoulder
> and speaks gently)

You dog! Don't ever do it again, but if you do, do it in better
verse.

Coleridge: Charles Lamb, I am ashamed of you.

Mrs. Kelly: You see, Baby, even *he's* ashamed of him.

Charles: (Still to Coleridge) You be hanged!

> (Sincerely)

But your face, when you repeat your verses, has all its ancient glory. An archangel—slightly damaged.

Mary: (Re-enters) Do come, Thomas.

> (Laughing gently at his dilemma)

Bring him with you.

> (De Quincey goes and Hazlitt after him. Coleridge fol-
> lows. Mrs. Kelly goes off. Charles and Fanny onstage
> alone)

Fanny: (Rushing to Charles) Oh, Charles, hasn't it been awful?

Charles: Oh, my friends are at their best tonight!

Mary: (Re-enters, and Charles and Fanny quickly drop their
hands. Mary is nervous) Charles, will you please come in
and help me? Oh, I'm sorry.

> (Fanny goes in quickly and Charles slowly follows, but as
> he is just about to enter into the inner room, George Dyer
> re-enters from the left wing)

Charles: Why George, what's the matter?

Dyer: I think, sir . . . I think I have left one of my shoes
behind.

> (He puts his books on the floor and leans the Bedlam can-
> vas against a chair)

Ah, yes, here it is.

> (Retrieves the shoe)

I must set forth again immediately. This time I shall discharge
your errand. It has not escaped my memory, I assure you.

Charles: (Solemnly kidding him, the needling that comes from
infinite tenderness) George, let me shake your hand. You
have transcended yourself.

(Dyer puts the shoe in his left hand and they shake hands)
You went half across London before you noticed one of your
shoes was missing?

Dyer: I was savoring the defense of the poet Menander.

Charles: Oh, George, George! Sometimes I think you are the
only one of us with both feet on the ground—shoes or no.
All the rest of us are at sea and sinking.

Dyer: The sea, sir, is a most unpredictable element and in certain cases virtually a cruel one.

Charles: George, yours is the most revolutionary conception
since Isaac Newton was smacked smartly on the head with
an orange.

Dyer: An orange? My memory grows less faithful daily. I could
have vowed that, in the case of Newton, the catalytic substance was an apple.

Charles: I was trying you out, George, as a test of your memory. It is more tenacious than you credit it. Tell me, how has
it been revealed to you that the sea is an unpredictable
element?

Dyer: This afternoon, sir, while on my accustomed stroll, the
stroll from which I returned here to be assisted from my
shawl through the kind offices of Miss Fanny Kelly, I encountered a brother-in-law of one of my nephews. He told me a
strange and harrowing epic of the waves.

Charles: Your memory, as you see, is in fine fettle. Now could
you recall this harrowing epic?

Dyer: There was a ship that lately foundered. It seems that the
ship's captain, a man of many voyages, was returning to his
native shores with a rich cargo. The heavens had been quite
mild when suddenly arose a storm of some fury. The gallant
skipper, ever ready to spring to the helm, on his way to that
post, stopped in the cabin at the invitation of several commercial gentlemen traveling as passengers.

Charles: Stopped, no doubt, to pray.

Dyer: One of the commercial gentlemen had with him certain
  bottles of brandy. It seems that when a bottle had been
  finished, our noble sea dog undertook to open a further
  bottle. While he was engaged in the task, the ship sank.
      (Charles bursts into laughter)
  You find this comical, sir?

Charles: (He picks up a bottle and a corkscrew and re-enacts
  the gesture as if he cannot believe it) Our noble sea dog took
  this further bottle, and while he was engaged in drawing the
  cork?—

Dyer: The ship sank.

Charles: (A fresh burst of laughter) You mean, the gallant
  skipper noticed nothing seriously amiss.

Dyer: Apparently not, sir.

Charles: But the water must have been—
      (Pantomimes shoulder depth)
  He did not notice the furniture floating around the cabin?

Dyer: It would seem not, sir.

Charles: (Wiping his eyes with a handkerchief) Oh, George,
  George, oblige me by living forever.
      (Sits, exhausted. There is a sudden uproar from within.
      Coleridge's voice is heard above it all)

Mary: (Rushes in from the inner room) Charles! Coleridge has
  gone wild! Coleridge is reading aloud from your "Confessions
  of a"—Oh, stop him!

Charles: (Rushing toward the door) Coleridge! No! No!

Coleridge: (He comes into the room before Charles reaches the
  door. He is in his declamatory mood. He is almost hypno-
  tized by his admiration for Charles' writing and the sound of
  his own voice) Oh, Charles, why didn't you tell me? Why
  didn't you let me read?
      (Charles falls back in horror as he sees Mrs. Kelly enter
      after Coleridge, her suspicions finally confirmed. Mary
      draws near Charles protectively)
  The style! The images! The rhythm!
      (Coleridge now reads from the magazine with great rolling
      tones)
  "Confessions of a Drunkard." "Why should I not declare that
  the name of the man of whom I speak is myself?"
      (Coleridge looks up from the magazine)

Oh, God, what courage! What sacrifice!

Charles: Coleridge, have you lost your mind? Stop!

Mrs. Kelly: (She is vindictive now) It's a fabulous character, isn't it, Mr. Lamb? Just a joke.

Coleridge: Listen! "There are those whom scarce any excess can hurt. I have seen them drink brandy like water. On them this discourse is wasted. They would but laugh at a weak brother. I speak to the nervous, the weak . . ."

Mrs. Kelly: Nervous and weak.

Coleridge: And the horror here!

(Reading again)

"An object of compassion to friends, of derision to foes, suspected by strangers, stared at by fools—"

Charles: Mrs. Kelly, you don't understand. You don't understand. It's a sickness, a terrible sickness. I have come back to health. I'm cured.

Mary: Can't you realize what his fight has been?

Mrs. Kelly: I realize that he has told everyone his shame about his nights of madness. I heard him read

(She indicates Coleridge)

"A man feels himself going down a precipice with open eyes and a passive will." A fine man, Mr. Lamb, a fine man that is. A man good enough for my daughter, I suppose.

Charles: I wrote this before I knew your daughter. I wrote it to try to tell England that drunkards are neither fearsome, nor comic. That they are miserable men; unfit, beleaguered—sick.

Mary: He is only saying that they must have understanding and help.

Mrs. Kelly: (Wheeling on Mary) Yes, just like you say about lunatics. You certainly both know what you're talking about.

Mary: Yes. We both do.

Mrs. Kelly: (Turning back to Charles) A fine family for a mother to see her daughter married into. If that's what you dared think I'd let her do.

Charles: Yes, I have dared.

Mrs. Kelly: (In a strident voice she calls to the inner room) Fanny! Fanny, come in here.

(She turns on Charles again)

The insolence! You, a drunken little nobody. A clerk!
(Fanny enters; Hazlitt follows)
With a sister a raving lunatic that London knows and points
at. A miserable idiot that should've been in Bedlam long ago.
(Mary takes it without flinching. She thinks only of
Charles)

Fanny: Mother! Mother!

Dyer: (Rising. To Mrs. Kelly) Madam, I will not stay and hear
Miss Lamb traduced.

Charles: You shame me, George.

Mrs. Kelly: Traduced? I'm sick of your fancy words. Do you
think they can hide the black sin in this house? Do you think
you can cover up what all London knows? This woman
(She accuses Mary point-blank)
is a murderess who's cheated the gallows.
(Charles turns toward Mary wildly, fearful of the results of
Mrs. Kelly's speech)

Mary: (Soothing Charles) Stay quiet, my dear, stay quiet.

Charles: (Turns on Mrs. Kelly in fury) Say what you will
against me, but you say another word about my sister and
I'll throw you down the stairs of this house.

Fanny: (Shrieking) Charles, what are you saying?

Mrs. Kelly: This *house*? This rat's nest of drunkards and lunatics and divorced men
(Hazlitt flinches)
and laudanum drinkers.
(Coleridge flinches)

Dyer: They also happen to be great artists, Madam.

Fanny: Charles, why have you done this?

Charles: I? I did this? There's no blame to that screeching hag
out of Hell?

Mary: (Pleading) Charles. Stay quiet, my dear. Please.

Fanny: Charles, if you dare say such things, I'll leave this place
forever.

Charles: (Sarcastic) Ah, the great speech. Shouldn't there be
something in it about "never darkening these doors again"?
Oh, excellently played. The great emotional actress doing
her biggest scene in a Loverpool stock company. In her greatest success: "The Mother Victorious," or "'Tis Pity She's a
Bitch."

Fanny: (Hurt) Charles, oh, Charles.

Mrs. Kelly: (To Fanny) Come out of here.

>(They exit. Charles is numbed and exhausted after the scene and walks slowly toward the table where he pours himself a brandy)

Dyer: Sir, Mrs. Kelly has been your guest; therefore, I do not like to speak ill of her. But never in the pages of literature have I encountered such an ungenerous, old . . . *sow*!

>(Mary has gone to comfort Charles)

Charles: Thank you, George.

>(Takes a large drink)

Well. What were we talking about before my life ended?

Dyer: (Searching) Sir, I'm much shaken. I am afraid I dare not trust my memory to serve us.

>(He starts off left. He stops and turns and picks up some of his books, forgetting the print of Bedlam, which is leaning against the chair. He turns to Charles)

Ah, yes! The sea. A harrowing epic. The tale of the ill-fated frigate, "Favorite."

Charles: *Favorite!!*

Dyer: Such was her name, sir. She carried a cargo of tea.

Charles: (He slowly collapses in a chair, his head goes down in his hands. In a moment he lifts his face, mirroring the grief and exhaustion. He speaks very slowly. Mary moves sympathetically to the back of his chair) And Coleridge said—then the gods reach for another thunderbolt.

>(Mary lays her cheek on the top of Charles' head. Dyer sits and puts on his shoe, stoops for his books, and starts off left. He turns and looks back at the scene; his shawl on the floor; the chair, the books, the print of Bedlam leaning against the chair. He makes a great effort to remember something. He cannot, and with a shake of his head he exits)

Hazlitt: Mary, ought we to go?

Mary: Yes, please. It's bad to ask you to leave our house. But just for now.

Coleridge: I can't forgive myself. I can't forgive myself.

Mary: You're forgiven. Coleridge, please?

>(Mary starts Coleridge and Hazlitt toward the door when De Quincey appears)

De Quincey: Mr. Coleridge?

Coleridge: Come, De Quincey.

(Coleridge, Hazlitt, and De Quincey go off)

Charles: (In a dull, hollowed voice) She's gone, Mary. Fanny's gone. Everything's gone.

Mary: (She returns to him in the chair and fondly pats his shoulder) Not everything, Charles. Charles, remember when you were a little boy? A little, little boy? A dove flew into our grandmother's garden. Oh, it was such a pretty thing. Its little shining head and its warm sweet body. Oh, you loved it so much and you wanted to keep it. I promised I'd help— and so together we started to build a little cage for it. We never finished it. When we came out the next morning your little dove had gone. Oh, Charles, you cried so hard. Your little heart was broken. But it healed again, Charles. Remember? Mary was there. Mary was always there.

(Charles pays no attention to her)

George has gone off without his shawl again.

(Goes to chair and picks up his shawl)

And he never yet found out the function of a book-shelf.

(Mary stoops and begins picking up the books and she suddenly sees the Bedlam canvas. She recoils sharply and whispers)

Bedlam!

Charles: (Musing about the recent scene with the Kellys) That that woman could say what she did to you.

Mary: (She turns to Charles numbly. Recollecting slowly) What did she . . . ?

(Remembering what Mrs. Kelly said, remembering that it did upset her)

Why, I didn't . . . I didn't think of it . . . I . . . I was thinking of you.

(Her fright disappears. She begins to surge, to come to the full height of her victory)

I can look at it now because I am not going there.

(Triumphant that at last the courage and strength come from within herself, she goes over to the canvas and picks it up)

I am never going to be there.

(Mary goes up to the back wall and hangs the Hogarth
"Bedlam" there and then slowly comes back down to her
former station behind Charles' chair)

Curtain

ACT THREE

Time: The time is a Thursday night, a week later.
Scene: The scene is the same as in the previous acts.

The lights, including the interior room, are subdued; many
of the candles are unlit; others are burned out. The room is
forlorn, chilled; the furniture, the whist table and chairs,
are in a state of disorder, and from the quantities of used
brandy and gin jugs on the table, liquor cabinet, even the
floor, it is obvious that the room has been the scene of a
protracted and desperate and lonely drinking bout by
Charles. The back wall holds all the Hogarths; the eighth
one, of Bedlam, hangs in the center of the wall above the
fireplace where Mary hung it in the last scene. As the curtain rises, Charles is on the stage alone. He is bedraggled. He
paces up and down before the buffet table in a frenzy. In a
moment he walks to the door to the inner room and shouts.

Charles: Emma!
   (Louder)
Emma!
   (Emma replies from within)
What time is it?
   (Again Emma replies from within)
   (Charles resumes his pacing, again tries to get another
   drop out of several of the jugs. He drops the last jug and
   renews his desperate pacing again)
Where in God's name has that idiot gone?
   (There is a knock on the door and Charles halts in terror
   of the sound. The knock repeats loudly. Emma enters from
   the inner room to answer it)
Don't answer it!
Emma: But it might be—
Charles: I know quite well who it is; it's East India House send-
   ing around its spies again. I shouldn't have sent them word I
   was sick; I should've said I was dead.
Emma: (She is almost frightened of him) But you *are* sick,
   Uncle Charles. Look, you're shaking.
Charles: Yes, child, I'm sick. An illness of my own procuring.
   Who is perfect?

(He paces again. Rather severely to Emma)
What time is it?

Emma: Why, it's perhaps a minute later than when I told you before.

Charles: (Lashing at her) Answer me! I said, "What time is it?"

Emma: Why, Uncle Charles! It's just past nine.

Charles: Oh, *where* is George?

Emma: (Cautiously beginning to tidy up the buffet table; she lifts some empty jugs) I'll take some of these away.

Charles: Oh, let them be! Stop your damned fretting and clattering.

(Emma drops her hands, breaks into tears, and runs off to inner room)
Oh, splendid! Now I've wounded a poor orphan child.

Becky: (Entering from the scullery, she intercepts Emma's flight, soothes her, and turns bitterly towards Charles)
Haven't you got anything better to do?

Charles: I'm sorry, Becky. I'm sorry, Emma.

Becky: Why don't you go out and get some air on those London streets you talk so much about? You haven't set foot out of this house for a week—God knows it looks it!

Emma: Uncle Charles is sick.

Becky: Sick! Brandy-sick and gin-and-water-sick.
(Cleaning up, hands bottles to Emma)
Here, take these out.
(Emma does)
Think shame of yourself, Charles Lamb.

Charles: I do, I do.

Becky: Pretty goings on, night and day in here with a bottle and your poor sister all worried and worn out with your filthy ways. Look at you, mooning around here about that actress with paint on her face. She never cared anything for you anyway; just wanted to get her name in the papers.

Charles: Oh, stop your damned blabbing.

Becky: You're not talking to Emma now. I'll stop nothing. I'll tell you what I think and, what's more, you'll listen to it. Hasn't your poor sister got enough without this nonsense of yours? Where's your spine? Where are your guts?

Charles: I haven't got any.

Becky: And the poor thing has always been so sweet and patient with you.

Charles: I know she is, I know she is. She's sweet, she's patient,
she's wonderful, and oh! I wish to God she'd give me something to hate her for.

Becky: Fine talk, that is; and about your own sister. And you,
all she's got in the world.

Charles: I know. And it is a heavy business being the only
thing that somebody's got in the world.

(Emma re-enters cautiously, eavesdropping)

You get tired. I'm so tired, and growing more tired every day
of these nine scurvy years . . . Ever since that day I came
home and wrenched the dripping knife out of her hand.

Emma: (To Becky) Is he talking . . . is he talking about the
terrible thing that happened with the knife?

(Bloodcurdling whisper)

Was it blood that was dripping off it?

Becky: (Wearied) Oh, be quiet, child, be quiet.

(There is a knock on the door)

Charles: Don't answer it.

Becky: I'll answer it. You can't hide in a corner here forever,
and people banging the door down.

(She goes off to answer the door)

Emma: (Gingerly) Uncle Charles, when I get old enough, will
you tell me what happened with the knife?

Charles: I'll tell you. I'll tell you. It slit a human throat! And I
wished to Christ it had been mine.

(Emma cowers)

Becky: (Handing him the envelope) Here, from East India
House.

Charles: (Takes it from her) From J. Wilberforce, Esquire, by
hand.

(He tosses it on the mantelpiece without opening it)

Becky: Well, don't stand gawking at it. Open it!

Charles: I know well enough what's in it. I don't want to see
the words.

Becky: (With another scornful glance at Charles, she shakes
her head hopelessly and starts toward the scullery. To
Emma) Here, some more, child.

(She hands her a few more bottles. Becky and Emma exit
to the scullery. George Dyer enters from left doubling
under his burden of jugs. Charles rushes toward him, feverishly taking the brandy away from him)

Charles: God, man, where'd you go for it, Land's End?

Dyer: I observed all reasonable haste.

Charles: (Tearing the bottle open) Lord help the man who
must depend on a creature like you to fetch him a drink he's
dying for.
(Pours liberal drink)

Dyer: (Pained) I can do no more than my best.

Charles: Forgive me, George. I have been so beleaguered with
horrors I no longer know what I do or say. No matter how
much I have offended you, you cannot hate me as I loathe
myself. God, why does the drunkard always turn on those
dearest to him?

Dyer: There is no hatred in me—only it saddens me, sir, that
these ways—

Charles: (Drinking) I know, I know—

Dyer: So worry your dear sister.

Charles: (Bitterly) Oh, what a couple we are! She in her constant danger, driving me to this; I with my stinking drunkenness sending her quicker to her hells. Two shipwrecked souls.
(Bitterly)
Like "Twelfth Night," isn't it? A brother and sister shipwrecked off the coast of Illyria.

Dyer: I dare not believe, sir, that things are as hopeless as you
see them.

Charles: Listen, my friend, I have spent too long seeing hope
when there could be no hope. Hopes that Mary might be
cured . . . hopes that my writings would one day earn
enough to purchase our safety . . . hopes of having the life of
a man, not a brother . . . hopes of Fanny—no word from her,
not a word—and I've even been a failure as a dreamer. What
dreamer could stand twenty years at East India House;
twenty years, with a pension always just ahead of me like a
carrot waved in front of a tired jackass! Through it all, over
and under everything, day and night, the need of money.
Money to pay my debts; money for Mary's care.

Dyer: Never before has the want of money made me miserable.

I wonder what sum I might realize from the sale of my Greek Testament.

Charles: (A wan smile) God bless you, George.

Dyer: It would be but a modest sum, I know, but perhaps added to other sums contributed by your friends—and I assure you, sir, they are your true friends.

Charles: My true friends are poor, George, like all true friends.

Dyer: Could you not cast yourself upon the mercy of East India House?

Charles: I've cast myself out of a job there by now.

(He gestures to the unopened letter on the mantelpiece)

Dyer: Oh, surely no! Even such men as your employers must have hearts.

Charles: Hearts! I had a fellow clerk named Tommy Blye. Thirty years he had worked there. One day he came an hour late, dizzy with fever. They cut his yearly wage to a third of what it had been. An hour late he was! I've not been there in a week. It was a week ago Fanny left. I've written her letters beyond counting. But there's been no answer from her. So I have sought oblivion here; but it does not come from jugs. I have no will. It's dead. I murdered it.

Dyer: But you have your sister and her love for you.

Charles: I know, and mine for her. Our love for each other has been our torment. It has condemned us both to an eternity of dual loneliness. How many times I have watched her suffer. How many times I wished she were dead.

Mary: (Enters from the inner room as Charles drinks. She tries to carry things off, but this sight makes her nervous. She begins to set things straight at the table, etc.) Oh, Charles, must you?

Charles: Tell me not and I doubly must!

Mary: We must make the place tidy. We have made small preparation for a Thursday night.

(To Dyer)

I hope, for Charles' sake, we will have guests.

Charles: Guests! There never was any poor devil as overguested as I am. If you know anybody who wants friends, George, I can spare him plenty. He shall have them good and cheap.

Mary: When you have these glooms you only think you are

outraged by the presence of people. And then when they
come you are far worse abused if they do not stay with you
till morning.

(Persuading tenderly)

You've been at home too much this week. It's such a pleasant night, why don't you go for a walk?

(To Dyer)

Charles and I were great walkers; we used to think nothing
of ten miles.

Charles: No, I have no wish to go out.

Mary: You're only saying that out of thoughtfulness for me.
You must not feel obliged to stay with me, Charles. I can
spare you for an hour or so; after all, I am always here.

Charles: God knows you are!

(Taking another desperate drink)

Can't you leave me alone? Can't you stop hanging over me?
Will you understand that I am not the little brother that you
have to comfort and pamper and protect? I want no more of
your damned wet-nursing.

Mary: Charles, you're weary.

Charles: For Christ's sakes, stop making excuses for me. Quit
your bloody everlasting patience.

Dyer: (Horrified at overhearing this, he raises a restraining
hand) My dear sir!

Mary: Of course you are weary, my dear. Forgive me, but
brandy only makes you wearier.

Charles: There! There, you see, you start it again—Oh, I'm
sorry, Mary. But this

(Indicating the brandy)

is the only rest.

Mary: Oh, it's not a good rest, Charles. Good tired comes after
work and then rest is good rest because you've earned it. I
thought we were going to be the way we were. I thought we
were going to be together again. Even to work together. Ah,
we should finish the Shakespeare tales!

(Pride)

You know, Charles, I've been able to work alone these last
few days. I've finished "As You Like It."

Charles: Good, good.

Mary: I've been so much stronger ever since I could . . .
  (A look to the Bedlam over the mantelpiece)
  look at that picture. Oh, I think I'm all cured—all well!
  Still, it's much better when we work together, Charles. Can't
  we try for a little while now? You know, sitting across the
  table from each other—"Darby and Joan," you used to
  call us.

Charles: Can't you see I can't work anywhere, anytime, now?
  Oh, Mary, can't you leave off your coaxing?

Mary: I cannot please you, Charles. I'm sorry. I thought it
  would be different.

Charles: That is everybody's epitaph.

Mary: Oh, I thought that I might be able in some little, little
  way to make up to you for Fanny—for what you've lost.
  But—Oh, anyway,
  (She sweeps her hand indicating the room's appearance)
  we can be better than this. We must be better than this.
  Charles, why don't we give this up? Why don't we go live in
  the country? There's Enfield, where my nurse lives. It's so
  quiet there and you could take long walks.
  (To Dyer)
  Oh, he was such a dauntless walker.

Charles: Mary, of course we couldn't do it.

Mary: (With difficulty) Then maybe *I* could go to live there
  and then you'd be free—and I'd be fine, really, Charles. Per-
  haps I could even have a little garden.
  (Panic)
  But you would come to see me often, Charles, wouldn't you?
  It isn't far.

Charles: Mary, this is fantasy.

Mary: Then could we go away for a few days?
  (Feverishly)
  To Cambridge! I have always wanted to see Cambridge.
  You've told me so much about it. We could go there alone,
  Charles. Alone together; with nobody's woes to fret us. Oh,
  please, couldn't you borrow a holiday and then we could
  both escape this London weariment.

Charles: My holidays are over and my borrowings ended.

Mary: Oh, Charles, do let us go to Cambridge. We would take

no care of time. We'd wander about and hunt for the little
autumn violets and watch the sun go down and the moon
rise. Alone together, Charles.

Charles: Ah, Mary, what a couple we are to go a-gypsying.

(Knock on the door. Charles looks again at the
mantelpiece)

Well, the letter's come, what have I to lose? I can answer any
door.

(To the door, left)

Mary: Oh, be like yourself again, Charles. Please make your
terrible pun. That dreadful "knock-eternal" one.

(Coleridge enters first. He goes silently to a chair and wea-
rily sinks there. Hazlitt follows closely, wiping his waistcoat with a kerchief. Charles brings up the rear, surveying
the scene with a bitter humor)

Oh, Coleridge, what has Wordsworth said to you now?

Coleridge: No one man can hurt me anymore; I am too deeply
wounded by all the world.

Hazlitt: (Dolefully shaking his head) Comrade!

Charles: (As Mary hesitates a moment) Pray go on. They've
just dropped in for the laughs.

Mary: Why, Hazlitt, weren't you to go to the theater? Oh, a
Thursday night and nothing prepared! Thank Heavens,
there's mutton in the scullery.

Hazlitt: (Swabbing himself with the kerchief) I was going! I
was actually on my way! Oh, Mary, Mary, how can I bear
this pain?

Charles: The Thursday evening bleat!

(Moves up, glass in hand. Savagely)

Why don't you leave us alone?

Mary: Charles, please; he's in trouble.

Charles: He thinks he is.

Mary: It's the same thing.

Hazlitt: As I was walking down the streets—alone with my
broken heart—a hackney coach came roaring at me. Hearing the sounds of ribald laughter coming from it, I thought
it to be a band of drunken roisterers and threw myself against
the wall to avoid their mad charge. My natural indignation
at this flouting of life and property turned to horror when I

saw, seated in this pagan chariot and laughing like a tipsy whore, none other than she who had once sworn to be true to me. And beside her, that lout! that clod! that *pig* of a commercial traveler! Look, see the mud they cast on me. This is the worst day of my life!

Charles: It seems to have been much like your other days.

Mary: (To Hazlitt) Here, let me have your waistcoat; I'll clean it for you.

Hazlitt: No, let it be. The earth from her wheels is fit covering for my dead heart.

Charles: (Savagely) Oh, Christ, Hazlitt, hang a wreath on your waistcoat and close your mouth!

Hazlitt: Why, Charles!

Mary: Try not to pay attention to him, Hazlitt. He's eaten with misery—and brandy.

Hazlitt: You hear him sneer at my sufferings?

(Laughs)

What does he know? What ache is there in his heart? He jests at scars that never felt a wound.

Coleridge: (Faintly noticing the room's drabness) It seems dark in here, or is it that everything seems dark to me? Where is Miss Kelly?

Mary: (Quickly) She is not here tonight.

(Changing subject)

How much young De Quincey admired you, Coleridge. Have you seen him since last Thursday?

Coleridge: All the time.

(With a thumb over his shoulder)

He will be here. He follows.

Charles: He *eats* his opium, doesn't he?

Coleridge: He says that the tincture of laudanum is unwholesome. It has alcohol in it.

Mary: (Gently) Coleridge, I had a most touching letter from your wife. She was saddened that you did not come home for your little boy's birthday.

Coleridge: His birthday?

Mary: Yes, a fortnight ago.

Coleridge: Oh, well. Next year.

(Mary has gathered plates to go to the scullery. Hazlitt

aids her. As they start moving toward the scullery, Mary
bursts out feverishly)

Mary: You know, Hazlitt, Charles and I are planning a trip to
Cambridge. I've always wanted to see Cambridge. I've never
seen it. We'll go by stagecoach. The Cambridge coach leaves
from Fetter Lane at eight o'clock. We'll go outside. High up,
like flying. We'll travel in the open air the way I used to go
on the stagecoach to my grandmother's.

(Mary and Hazlitt exit into the scullery)

(Knock on door)

Coleridge: (Drearily) That will be Junior.

Charles: George, will you please?

(Dyer closes his book and goes to the door. There is a moment's pause as Charles surveys the jug in his hand, and
then he speaks to Coleridge harshly)

A brilliant Thursday night at the Lambs'. Coleridge!

(Coleridge slowly lifts his head)

Do you remember one Thursday night—I had stopped my
drinking and you had stopped your—

(Gestures)

Coleridge: Yes, I've strung that broken vow on my rosary.

De Quincey: (Precedes Dyer into the room. He starts toward
Charles but pauses a moment behind Coleridge's chair and
speaks reproachfully to him) Ah, Mr. Coleridge, you said
you'd wait for me.

(Coleridge groans)

Is there anything wrong, Mr. Lamb?

Charles: (Bitterly) Oh, no, no—what could be wrong here?

Mary: (Enters with a tray of veal pies) Hazlitt is telling Emma
about his poor broken heart. He is also eating a considerable
portion of mutton. Why, good evening, Thomas. Oh, do help
me out. Try our veal pie and see if it's as good as we hope
it is.

De Quincey: Oh, no, Miss Mary, I've eaten.

Mary: Now what did you eat and when did you eat it?

De Quincey: Half a roll, this morning; a fairly large roll.

Mary: But just taste this as a special favor to me.

(Fills his plate)

De Quincey: Is Miss Kelly to be here tonight?

Charles: No! Miss Kelly will not be here tonight! Miss Kelly will not come any more to this god-damned stable of nightmares.

(He exits to the inner room)

Mary: (Turns to De Quincey desperately and speaks to him, now "between inspiration and possession") Thomas, have you ever been to Cambridge? In my life I've never spent so many pleasant hours as Charles and I did there. We congratulated ourselves that we had come alone. We wanted all our hours greedily to ourselves. But we met such a pleasant undergraduate. We took him to our inn for dinner. We had tea with him. It was such a delicious college room. Then again he supped with us. He was so easy with us; he didn't know I was different from anybody else. We made our meals as short as possible to lose no time and then went out to walk again. Charles showed me Jesus College, where Coleridge was—I peeped in at his window.

(Coleridge starts)

You have seen the little churches in Cambridge, Thomas? You cannot go a mile without starting a steeple with its little patch of villagery around it. Bless the little churches, how pretty they are!

De Quincey: When did you make your visit, Miss Lamb?

Mary: Oh, this last week. My brother borrowed a holiday from East India House.

(Again she is suddenly tranquil)

It's a drab Thursday but we still have our cold mutton. Will you come in and try it?

(Mary leads De Quincey and Coleridge to the door of the inner room. She turns and ushers them through and then speaks to Dyer)

George, do come eat.

Dyer: I have one page to complete in this volume. I could not in any courtesy leave the author so abruptly.

(Mary leaves)

Fanny: (She enters from the left, unannounced. She is penitent; ill-at-ease. She cannot be sure of how she will be received in the house. She is relieved to see Dyer sitting there alone)

Mr. Dyer.

Dyer: (Delighted to see her) Miss Kelly! I bid you good
evening.

Fanny: (Stalling embarrassment) How are you?

Dyer: I am enjoying my usual rugged health.

Fanny: It's pleasant weather, isn't it? I mean, for this time of
year.

Dyer: Ah, you, too, are aware of the extraordinary benignity
of the season. I was saying only today that we are experienc-
ing less an English autumn than a Grecian spring. My
listener—whose appellation, I trust, will presently recur to
me—

(Taps his temple in an attempt to remember)
most agreeably conceded that he considered me to be
correct.

Fanny: Is Charles . . . is Mr. Lamb at home?

Dyer: Mr. Lamb has, I believe, sought his chamber. Oh, my
dear young lady, he has not been at all in good health these
past seven days.

Fanny: Oh! Is he ill? Has the apothecary been? Has he a fever?

Dyer: To my knowledge it has not been necessary to summon
medical assistance. Mr. Lamb is not confined to his bed. Indeed, the deplorable circumstance is that he finds no rest
there, nor otherwhere.

Fanny: Has he . . . did he . . . does he ever speak of me?

Dyer: My dear young lady, oh, my dear young lady, he does. He
speaks your name in sorrow; with, as Shakespeare has it,
rue. It appears to be his sad conviction that when you bade
him farewell last Thursday you did so in finality. I have not
yet abandoned my own hope that he is afflicted with confusion on this subject. Will you not encourage me to hope that
I am not overly impudent in my opinion?

Fanny: Oh, Mr. Dyer, you're not. You're not.

Dyer: He would be, if I may use so strong a word, distraught
did he know you were here present and he not cognizant of
your coming. May I not acquaint him with the fact of your
nearness?

Fanny: (Imploring) Oh, please.

Dyer: Splendid! I beg you to excuse me.

(He exits through the door to the inner room)

Fanny: (She looks about the room fondly. She sees the figurines on the mantelpiece. They are looking away from each other. She makes a gesture toward them and then checks herself) Oh, I'm sorry. I forgot.

(Charles enters from the door to the inner room. Fanny rushes to him)

Oh, Charles. Oh, Charles. You're ill. You shouldn't be up!

(They embrace)

What can you think of me?

Charles: What I have always thought of you—doubled now.

Fanny: (Touching his face tenderly) Oh, poor Charles, you *are* ill.

Charles: I must be. I must be fevered. I seem to see Fanny Kelly. I seem to be touching her lovely hands. Never to hear from you all this week.

Fanny: All this thousand years. I thought I had died with no word from you. I found that was death for me, Charles.

Charles: Death for me when you left and then down into Hell the rest of these days.

Fanny: Charles, I didn't know about your letters to me. This is hard for me to say. Mother . . . Mother had answered every knock at the door. She had taken your letters. Our little maid told me today.

(Wryly)

Mother, thank God, was at the milliner's. I ransacked our rooms. I ripped her bed down to the mattress. God help me, I tore up the carpets. I went beside myself, Charles. And then I opened the chest for a handkerchief for my frantic tears and there, under her fluted caps, all sprinkled with lavender —I hate the smell of it!—were the letters you had sent to me.

Charles: She did not burn them? I thought her a woman of fire.

Fanny: Charles, don't now. I've been grateful to her. I've tried to hold it always in my mind I must be loyal to her. But she's not been loyal to me. To keep your letters from me, that was to shield not me but herself.

Charles: Fanny, don't talk about it anymore. The centuries in Hell, this week . . . and this moment's touch of your fingertips, right into Paradise.

Fanny: Oh, Charles, were you so ill?

Charles: (He's gay now) My dear, when you first came in my head was playing all the tunes in the world; ringing such peals. It had finished "Merry Christ Church Bells" and was beginning "Turn Again Whittington." Didn't you hear?

Fanny: Not a sound.

Charles: Ah, you should've kept quiet. Thank God, you didn't!

Fanny: Your sister, Charles?

Charles: I've distressed her only less ill than I have distressed myself.

Fanny: How badly we humans are designed. Distressment in one of us and those about us fall like tenpins.

(There is an authoritative knock on the door)

Charles: (Leading Fanny to a chair) Stop looking like a visitor. Sit down. Sit down.

(The knock is repeated)

Oh, for God's sakes!

(Raises his voice)

Oh, come in, the door's off the latch. Your hand's too soft for the pushing? Then blow upon our portal as a child does on a dandelion fluff and join us all unwelcome.

(Mr. Wilberforce enters. He enters from the door left. He is a spare man, cold and imperious. He is dressed in black. He is rather sinister)

Wilberforce: Lamb.

Charles: (Shaken at the sight of him) Oh, God, I forgot. I forgot food and water and rent. I forgot our living.

Wilberforce: Lamb.

Charles: (In a tone which says: "What can I lose?") Good evening, Mr. Wilberforce. Miss Kelly, this is Mr. Wilberforce.

(Fanny curtsies. Wilberforce bows. Bitterly)

A little deeper, both of you. This is Miss Fanny Kelly of Drury Lane and this is the Director-in-Chief of East India House.

Wilberforce: Miss Kelly, this is a pleasure. I have witnessed various of your performances at the Drury Lane, and I am enlisted forever in the ranks of your followers.

(Fanny makes a deep curtsy. Wilberforce bows again. Wilberforce clears his throat)

And now, sir, to our business.

Charles: (Aside to Fanny) Take a deep breath and count ten.

Wilberforce: I have tried to communicate with you for several days, as you know.

Charles: As I know.

Wilberforce: I have been grieved to learn of your continued illness. You are not, as a matter of fact, looking well.

Charles: As I know.

Wilberforce: However, you will have ample opportunity to recover now that you are relieved of your labors at East India House.

Fanny: Oh! Oh, no!

Charles: My gratitude for this gift of leisure is in conflict with my indecision as how best to use it. Would you suggest a tour of Germany, a dash to Paris, or is this the season for the Italian lakes?

Wilberforce: I think some place of seclusion where you may recover your health.

Charles: Such as debtors' prison.

(Wilberforce expresses pain)

I'm sorry, I can take no more of this.

Wilberforce: (Puzzled) I trust you will take my congratulations.

(Heavily playful)

Since you could not come to East India House, East India House has come to you.

Charles: Please stop this game.

Wilberforce: Game? East India House never takes part in games. Do you think my letter to you was in jest? The letter was delivered to you, was it not?

Charles: Oh, yes, it was delivered. There it is.

(Points to mantelpiece)

Wilberforce: (Goes and picks up letter) But it is still sealed!

Charles: Oh, to hell with the heavy paper and the seal and the fine words above it. When a man is sacked, let him be sacked without the indecencies of formality.

Wilberforce: (Breaks the seal of the letter and exposes a sheaf of bank notes. Charles takes them, thunderstruck) You are indeed a sick man!

Charles: What in God's name is this?

Wilberforce: That, sir, is the first quarter's payment of the pension awarded you by the directors of East India House.

(Reading the letter)

"In consideration of the many years of loyal and loving service—"

Charles: When? When?

Wilberforce: You became a gentleman of leisure a little less than a week ago. If I may say it, sir—

Charles: You may say anything.

Wilberforce: Thank you. It is unique in the annals of East India House that an employee should be granted a pension before he has served fifty years there. But in view of the august names in England's literary world that were signed to the petition—

(To Fanny)

E. I. H. has always been a patron of English letters—we felt it our noble obligation to accede to the request. We expect that our gift to you will facilitate your contribution to England's storehouse of literature. E. I. H.'s loss is literature's gain. Is that not so, Miss Kelly?

Fanny: Oh, I'm sure, sir.

Wilberforce: East India House considers it a privilege to pay a just reward. Well done, thou good and faithful servant.

(Shakes hand)

Again, my congratulations.

(Moving toward the door)

Charles: Thank you.

(As Wilberforce nears the door; almost beyond hearing)

Honey!

(Wilberforce exits)

Fanny: Oh, Charles, it's true! It's really true!

Charles: (Jubilantly) Of course, it's true. Everything that's good is true now. The darkness is gone and the stars are out.

(Embracing each other in joy. Becky and Emma enter from the scullery)

Becky! Emma! Look.

(Waves a sheaf of bills at them)

It's come! My pension's come! We've got it!

Becky: Oh, thank the dear Lord for this day.

Emma: (Streaking through the door to the inner room) Aunt
Mary! Aunt Mary! We're pensioned! Hell's froze over!
   (George Dyer enters. Charles rushes toward him)
Charles: May I have this waltz?
   (He turns the bewildered Dyer around and releases him so
   that Dyer staggers against the bookcases)
Pensioned, George, *pensioned*!
Fanny: (Excitedly) Oh, Mr. Dyer, isn't it beautiful? Oh, our
stars are out, Mr. Dyer.
   (To Becky)
Oh, Becky, bring in lots and lots of candles, won't you?
Becky: Indeed I will, my dear. There's not enough candles in
all London.
Fanny: There's no flowers and there ought to be flowers. Miss
Mary ought to have flowers. I'll go get some at the barrow at
the corner. I'll be right back, Charles.
   (She exits left)
Dyer: (He goes to his chair. Starts to sit) I am, sir, overcome.
Charles: (Catching him) Ah, no you don't. No basking for you
now like an Ethiop at noonday. There's work for you. Blithe
work. Listen!
   (Charles pulls a bill free and thrusts it toward Dyer)
Fly, O wood nymph, on thy rosy sandaled feet
   (He looks quickly at George's feet)
—sure you've got both your shoes on—fly to the nearest pub
for a thousand gallons of ineffably delicious brandy and float
right back here with it on the evening breeze.
   (Dyer starts to answer him but Charles cuts him off)
Yes, yes, I know you went before but this must not be rotgut,
my mischievous elf.
   (Dyer tries to leave but Charles prevents him)
Wait! Wait!
   (Hands Dyer another bill)
Hold on, wild stallion.
   (Hands him another bill)
Stop at the good Mr. Wink, the apothecary, where you will
find Coleridge taking on a cargo for a voyage to the moon—
No, no, I forgot, he's here. I want them all here, the old fa-
miliar faces.
   (Hands another bill)

Press coins on my mendicant friends in the gutters; Legless
Tom, Roaring Bess, and Dick the Fiddler. Pass no gin shop,
enter each. Count the heads, including those rolling on the
floor, and provide each with tuppence. Get on now, and
none of your stopping to sport with Amaryllis in the shade.
(Dyer leaves, dropping a bill; Charles rushes to the inner
room)
Mary! Emma! Hazlitt! Becky! Coleridge! De Quincey!
Emma: (Enters with long candles) Becky, Becky, bring more
candles. Light all the candles. Hell's froze over!
Mary: (Entering with Hazlitt, De Quincey and Coleridge) I
feel as if all tears have been wiped from my eyes and all
cares from my heart.
Hazlitt: Oh, Mary, this is the happiest day of my life.
Coleridge, come drink to the great occasion.
Coleridge: By Heaven, I will.
De Quincey: (Patiently warning him) Mr. Coleridge, alcohol is
injurious.
Hazlitt: (Drink in hand) To the new life for the Lambs. To
time and riches!
Mary: (Taking a glass) Time and riches. That's the right order.
Riches are only good because they afford us time.
(They drink the toast. Becky enters with candelabra)
Oh, good, Becky. Put one here—
(Indicates one side of the mantel)
and that one there. And Emma, set out the Hogarth glasses.
We must pay this night our highest compliment.
(There is a knock on the door)
Guests! And Charles will be glad of them now. Emma, their
coats and cloaks on the table in the hall.
(The first of the evening guests arrive. They are a hand-
somely dressed husband and wife. The woman, called Mrs.
Crittenden, is a remarkably pretty young woman. She goes
right to Hazlitt)
Mrs. Crittenden: Good evening, William.
Hazlitt: (Hazlitt forgets her name) Ah, yes—Good evening,
good evening. Miss Lamb, may I present Mr. and Mrs. . . .
ah . . .
Mrs. Crittenden: (Gushing) Oh, we've so looked forward to

meeting you. William—he's such a dear old friend of ours—
said that you were such a dear friend of his that he felt quite
free to invite us to come to a Thursday night. Any Thursday
night.

Hazlitt: I did?

    (His hand to his heart)

I must have been crazed with pain.

Mary: I'm so glad that you did come.

    (Waving toward Coleridge and De Quincey)

  Mr. Coleridge over there. And Mr. De Quincey.

    (Toward the buffet)

Won't you have something?

Mrs. Crittenden: It's so gay and pretty here.

Mary: It's a gay and pretty night.

Mrs. Crittenden: (Having caught Coleridge's eye, with a deep
curtsy) Oh, Mr. Coleridge . . .

Coleridge: (Brings her up from the curtsy very slowly. He
regards her with an appraising look) You . . . ah . . . live
near by?

Mrs. Crittenden: And this is my husband.

Coleridge: (Quite intent on Mrs. Crittenden) Perhaps I've been
too much away from London.

Mr. Crittenden: It is indeed an honor to meet Samuel Taylor
Coleridge.

Hazlitt: (Through his teeth) My dear old friend, your dear new
friend hates to be called Samuel.

Mr. Crittenden: Several times we have journeyed down to hear
Mr. Coleridge lecture, but he never appeared on the
platform.

Hazlitt: Well, they say he is somewhat eccentric.

Mary: Anything anybody can say about Coleridge is true.

Mrs. Crittenden: William said that Miss Fanny Kelly comes
here often.

Mary: (Quietly) She is not here tonight.

Mr. Crittenden: They say at times Coleridge can be the most
brilliant talker in the world.

Hazlitt: I once heard him talk for three hours without inter-
ruption. A magnificent volcano of language.

Mr. Crittenden: And what was his subject?

Hazlitt: Oh, I cannot tell you that, sir. I didn't understand one single syllable.

Dyer: (He enters from left. His clothes are torn as if he had been the victim of mob violence) I am returned.

Mr. Crittenden: Great grief! What is this?

Dyer: I have sought to carry out all the missions with which your brother has charged me.

> (Mary, despite the stir in the room at Dyer's appearance, cannot help a smile. As he puts the jugs on the table)

I am assured that these do not contain rotgut. I regret that I durst visit but one gin shop. Those there present did not at first believe genuine my offer of tuppence per head. Persuaded of my good faith, they not only snatched the monies but, when I left the shop, they trooped out after me to a man—and I regret to say, to a lady—and followed me through the streets urging all those they met to join the procession—if you will pardon the term, the decidedly ribald procession—and garner a share of the coppers. I fear, in their childlike enthusiasm, they have rudely disarranged my attire. They have made me, as you may conjecture, somewhat conspicuous.

> (Mary comes to him and leads him toward the door to the inner room)

I bid you good evening.

> (Mary ushers him through the door)

Mary: (To Crittenden) He writes, too.

Coleridge: (To Mary, as she approaches with more food for De Quincey) I've been telling De Quincey, I've prayed so long for this day that I thought it would never come. This will mean everything to Charles.

Mary: I hope so.

Coleridge: And to you, too, Mary. You'll have no more long days alone.

Mary: Oh, I so want us to go away—away from London. If we could get back to the old days, alone together. If we could go someplace where we would be like other people. Some place of sanctuary from memories and ghosts. Charles must have peace.

Coleridge: He has been in a sad state.

Mary: I thought it would be so right with Fanny. I did what I could but—Oh, I've got to help him. I must find the way to heal his deep new wounds. If I cannot aid him now then what good am I to him or myself?

Coleridge: (As Charles enters from the inner room, fresh in attire and spirit. Charles goes around the room greeting guests and comes up to De Quincey and Coleridge) Charles, we can drink the happiest toast of our lives.

Charles: I drink to my friends who signed the petition that gave me liberty.

Coleridge: Well, first let us drink farewell to East India House.

Charles: Farewell forever to the cursed desk. The desk and the grave, they are the same, save at the latter you are outside of the machine.

   (He has poured himself a glass of porter)

   Of course, I'll toast, but in malt beverage. I've no more need of brandy and I intend giving up tobacco soon.

Mary:'(Affectionately) Coleridge, your arms are longer than mine.

   (She gestures)

   Set his halo straight on him, will you?

Charles: And next week, we'll have roast pig instead of cold mutton. Won't we, Mary?

Mary: Yes, Charles.

Coleridge: You have had a gift from Heaven, Charles.

Charles: I've had a payment from Hell for twenty years service there!

Coleridge: At least Hell pays off her commercial men, but geniuses go always unpaid.

Hazlitt: The remuneration for genius is a murdered heart!

Charles: Enough! Mary, make them hush their bleating for tonight.

Mary: I'll take care of them, Charles.

Mrs. Crittenden: (To Mary) Most unusual, your picture collection, Miss Lamb.

Mary: Yes, it's "The Rake's Progress." We have the whole series, you see. The final one,

   (She indicates)

   here, I hung myself.

Mrs. Crittenden: Oh, I've heard of that one. It's the Bedlam
   scene, isn't it? Oh, the poor wretches.
Mary: (Explaining the details of the Bedlam scene) And these
   figures are sane and elegant ladies, smirking through their
   fans at the naked madman, rattling his chains in his agony.
Mr. Crittenden: Sad, sad sight.
Mary: And sad, sad, people; unwanted people.
   (Fanny enters from stage-left wing. She is lovely, her face
   animated. She carries an armful of flowers. Her entrance is
   a signal for everyone to turn, including the Crittendens. It
   is so timed that Mary, concentrating on the Bedlam scene,
   speaks one last line; nobody is paying any attention to her
   anymore)
   You see, these are the cast-offs. The ones with no one who
   loves them; with no family, with no brother to care for
   them.
Charles: (Delighted to see Fanny) Fanny!
   (Mary, losing the company's attention, moves quickly
   downstage toward Fanny. It is in a way a protective
   movement)
Fanny: Mary! Oh, Miss Mary,
   (She gestures to explain the flowers in her arms)
   these are for the celebration. Isn't it wonderful news?
Mary: (Unsettled at seeing Fanny again) Oh. Then you've
   heard it already.
Fanny: I was here. I was first to know.
Mary: (With a look at Charles, who is raptly watching Fanny)
   I thought I was the first to know.
   (To Fanny)
   Sisters are such selfish beings.
Fanny: (She relinquishes the flowers to Charles. He hands
   them to Mary without even looking at her) Oh, Charles.
   (Charles and Fanny look at each other. They are uncon-
   scious of the room around them)
Mr. Crittenden: Miss Kelly, may I tell you how much I have
   enjoyed your performances.
Fanny: (With an automatic smile) Thank you. You're very
   kind, sir.
   (Returns to Charles with double the attention, softly)

I do pray very well, don't I, Charles?

Charles: (As he turns her toward the door to the inner room)
And now I wonder how'll you be about answering a prayer?
(Charles and Fanny exit through the inner door)
(Mary goes to the bookcases and the flowers as Becky enters from the scullery with bread, bread board, and knife.
As Mary turns downstage toward Becky, she whispers)

Mary: Charles. Charles, please. Please, help me. Please, Charles.

Mr. Crittenden: Mr. Coleridge, we hope sometime to be successful in hearing you lecture, sir.

Coleridge: I find the lecture platform empty as to gratification and profitless as to guineas.

Mr. Crittenden: The worth of great words is not to be measured in guineas and pounds.

Hazlitt: (Bitterly) That is always a difficult matter to explain to the butcher.

Coleridge: (Ranting again) Butchers! Pounds! Guineas! The shackles on a poet's wrists, the whip across his back. Are we never to know freedom? Oh, to be born a genius is to be born accursed.

Mary: (She has reached the table near Becky and now whirls on Coleridge, knife in hand but almost not realizing she has it there) Oh, Coleridge, you and your shackles! You have all the freedom any man could take and it's made you its slave. What the Devil's the matter with you? What the Devil's the matter with all of you? I know I have defended your ridiculous behavior but I can find no further defense for it. You geniuses, charging about calling yourselves accursed and God Almighty; taking pride in the word. Calling yourselves lost, the whole generation of you, *lost*! Yet may God help the one who tries to rescue you. You don't want to be rescued. You want to stay lost, so you can be pitied for your weaknesses, and excused of your indulgences, and exempted from your moral taxes. Making your own rules for your own selves; too precious and free to obey the laws of human behavior. So filled with pity for yourselves that if there is another to be pitied you shrink away and cry, "Calamity!" Christ, if you knew what calamity means!

Hazlitt: Mary!

Mary: It means to live in dependence and fear. It means that
the love you give is a curse and the love you take is a
charity. Geniuses! Lost! Accursed! Running from life—
swooning if life comes near you. Who do you think you are?
Who the Devil do you think you are?

Mrs. Crittenden: Oh, dear, oh dear, oh dear!

Coleridge: (Aghast) Mary!

Mary: (Quieting) I've listened to you; I've listened to all of
you for years. And now I've talked for a minute.

Coleridge: Mary, Mary! You must not excite yourself so.

Mary: I'm quite tranquil, thank you.

  (She gives Coleridge a playful slap)

Well, I love you all for the good that's in you and look for no
change.

  (Becky takes the knife from Mary's hand without
  comment)

Becky: What about the hot punch, Ma'am? Now I've went and
made it; is it there's nobody going to drink it?

Mary: Oh, this is Becky's work of art! We cannot hurt her pride
in it. Please, you must all go in.

  (The Crittendens move toward the door to inner room.
  Coleridge, De Quincey, and Hazlitt follow them.
  As Mary waits upstage near the flowers, De Quincey
  comes up to her and, noticing the flowers, speaks to her
  tenderly)

De Quincey: How sweet and fresh.

Mary: Yes, she's so young, isn't she? And so lovely. Who could
blame him?

De Quincey: Once there was loveliness for me, too. Ann, her
name was.

Mary: (Gently) You knew each other when you were children?

De Quincey: No. We met in the streets of London when I first
came. We used to meet every night on our corner—we called
it our corner. She was my little sister, the one I had loved
. . . the one who had died. We used to talk all the nights
through, huddled together in doorways, in corners of empty
warehouses. She had no place to live, either. Once she saved
my life. I was far gone in fever, and she took her last pennies

and ran and brought me medicine. One night, she did not
come to our corner. I waited there night after night, but she
never came again.

Mary: You cannot find her?

De Quincey: No. She was all alone in the world. She made her
living in the streets. She was fifteen years old. I look and
look, but I do not know how to search. You see, I never
knew her last name.

Mary: Searching and never finding. To find her once, to find
happiness once, and then to lose it. How sorrowful! How
bitter! How nearly that happened to my Charles. Thank
Heavens, it will not.

> (Mary now changes the figurines back so that they face
> each other. Fanny and Charles enter and Mary and De
> Quincey come up to them)

Are you coming in, children?

> (Looks at them and then comes to them)

No, of course you're not. Come, Thomas.

> (Mary turns, takes Fanny's hand in her own and then
> Charles' hand in her other hand. She releases them
> tenderly)

I wish you happy.

> (Mary goes into the inner room, after De Quincey, closing
> the door behind her)

Charles: (He speaks to Fanny as if he has said all this before)
Don't you see how she feels? She loves us, Fanny, and she
wants our happiness.

Fanny: I think she does.

Charles: We can be so happy here.

Fanny: But Charles, again I ask you, who is "we"? "We" can be
only two.

Charles: You and I.

Fanny: Charles, can you really do this to her?

Charles: Fanny, we have a right to our own happiness. You
heard her wish it to us. She was speaking longingly of the
country only a while ago. There's Enfield. The soft, quiet
countryside, and her nurse is there and her friends will come
and we'd go often to be with her.

Fanny: I think she could do it. I think she would do it. But it is you; Charles, I don't know if you could. Do you realize this has been your life? It's been so long. It's gone so deep.

Charles: If I am happy, then she will be happy. She's like that.

Fanny: Yes, she's like that.

Charles: Dearest Fanny. Dearest love. Dearest life.

> (They start to embrace just as the door to the inner room reopens. Everyone has a glass of punch)

Hazlitt: Run for your lives, the floodgates have burst. Coleridge is talking.

Charles: (As the Crittendens enter, rather stunned) A genuine talent struggling against a pompous display of it.

Mr. Crittenden: (To Hazlitt) Was there ever a man so eloquent?

Hazlitt: And so troublesome with his eloquence.

Coleridge: (He enters with Mary and De Quincey. Mary is showing obvious signs of fatigue and nervousness) Now to take the other side, Luther said, and I think truly, how different a rich country is from a happy one. Rich countries are always unhappy, miserable, degraded countries.

Mary: (Distraught) People, too. Oh, people, too!

De Quincey: May I fetch you anything, Miss Lamb?

Mary: No, thank you, Thomas.

De Quincey: I've been watching you. You do too much for people.

Mary: There's not much left for me to do.

De Quincey: You're tired. I wish you could have a rest.

Mary: Perhaps I shall. Yes, I've been rather thinking of going away from London. Perhaps I shall go for a bit to Cambridge. I've never been there, you know.

> (Looking around her)

Oh, there's a cup wants filling.

> (She grows increasingly busy as the hostess. Entering into the inner room to refill punch glasses, seeing that the buffet is provident, all the while the growing weariness, the strain, becoming more and more obvious)

Hazlitt: (To Coleridge) The first sense you've spoken. Although you cannot expect me to agree when you imply that poverty is our solution.

Coleridge: I implied no such thing. How could I? But we are in a dreadful state. One class presses with iron foot upon the wounded heads beneath. We need most deeply a reform, but not the muddling reform we shall have. The system must alter. The system must alter radically, for to believe in the future one must be a radical. England has too long hidden her face from the future.

Mr. Crittenden: Brave talk, sir, but how could a radical change be effected?

Coleridge: Never an easy way. Always the hard, costly way.

Mr. Crittenden: (Almost sneering) As Russia threw off Bonaparte? And a thousand of her towns burned and pillaged, and the cream of her young men dead?

Coleridge: It is worth that cost, or any cost. God spare them another invader, ever, but if one should come, they must turn him back though it cost them their last village and their last young man.

Mrs. Crittenden: (Brightly) Well, they say that wars are a good thing, in a way. If they didn't have them, there'd be too many people.

Hazlitt: Peace would bring about such a fearful crush, wouldn't it?

Mary: (Making her last desperate efforts as a hostess) Oh, ladies and gentlemen, remember Charles' rule: No talk of war and politics. What about some whist?

(To De Quincey)

Come, Thomas, take a hand of whist.

De Quincey: Oh, Ma'am, I don't know how to play cards.

Mary: Well, whist is a game for such a few. Let's try for something we can all play. There is a fine game that Charles invented. It's called "What Persons Would You Like Most to Have Seen," and its name tells you how it's played.

Mrs. Crittenden: Oh, most interesting. Tell us how it's done.

Mary: You simply say what person you most wished to have seen and tell us the reason for your choice.

Mr. Crittenden: (To Hazlitt) What have the selections been as a rule?

Hazlitt: Oh, the obvious ones: Shakespeare, Jonson, Chaucer— with the obvious objections to all of them.

Mrs. Crittenden: (Archly to Hazlitt) None of my sex, dear William?

Coleridge: There is no need to summon back even the most
exemplary of ladies, for already we have in the room with us
(Bows to Mary)
one as gracious, as sensible, as virtuous as any that went
before her.

Mrs. Crittenden: Indeed! And who would this exemplary lady
choose?

Mary: I will ask for one of my sex. I should like vastly to have
seen Ninon de L'Enclos.

Charles: (Amazed) Why?

Mary: Because I have not seen anyone like her.

Charles: My sister, my incomparable sister! When Shakespeare
set a birthmark on a breast, she would not write of it until
she had chastely moved it to a cheek. And now she wants to
talk to a king's mistress.

Hazlitt: Charles, you haven't chosen yet?

Charles: Oh, I should choose Guy Fawkes. I should like to com-
miserate with him that his Gunpowder Plot did not take
effect.

Mr. Crittenden: Sympathy for treason? You'd have had him
blow up Parliament?

Charles: Ah, but think what a glorious explosion it would have
made.
   (Seriously)
No. I think I should like to have seen Judas Iscariot.

Mrs. Crittenden: (In horror) Mr. Lamb!

Charles: To see the face of him who could dip his hand in the
same dish as the Son of Man and afterwards betray him.

Hazlitt: What would you say to him?

Charles: I would not speak. I would kiss the hem of his garment, for he had once walked with the Savior.

Mary: Thomas, now you see how The Game is played, will you
take your turn?

De Quincey: I decided whom I wanted to see long before I
heard of the game. I had always chosen Cain.

Mrs. Crittenden: (Aghast) Cain!

De Quincey: Oh yes, as the inventor of murder and the father
of the art, Cain must have been a man of first-rate genius.

Mr. Crittenden: You endorse murder as a work of genius? You
  approve it?
De Quincey: Oh, only as an art. As a line of conduct I consider
  it highly improper and the result of incorrect thinking.
Coleridge: De Quincey, another time for your theories!
De Quincey: (Going on) Once a man indulges in murder, very
  soon he comes to think little of robbing, and from robbing he
  comes next to drinking and Sabbath breaking, and from that
  to incivility and procrastination. Once begin upon this
  downward path, you never know where you are to stop.
  Many a man dated his ruin from some murder or other that
  perhaps he thought little of at the time.
Mrs. Crittenden: You're like me. I just hate the idea of murder-
  ing. O-o-o, all that blood!
Hazlitt: Yes, it does play hob with the carpets.
Mr. Crittenden: We may be thankful that our courts deal
  promptly with fiends and murderers.
De Quincey: Oh, a moment, sir. Some of our murder trials are
  interminable. Take, for example, the case of Mary Blandy.
  Her trial is the perfect example of what Hamlet calls "the
  law's delay." Her defenders sought for months to excuse her
  on the ground that she was overset in her intellects but—
    (He shrugs)
  I had a friend who was fortunate enough to have seen her
  execution. On the scaffold she said, "Gentlemen, pray do not
  hang me high, for sake of decency." Think of that little light
  body hanging from a rope. Poor little Mary Blandy. Poor
  thing.
Mrs. Crittenden: (Mary is serving her at this moment) Poor
  thing, indeed! She should've been drawn and quartered. She
  murdered her mother!
    (Mary reels under this statement as if it were a tremen-
    dous physical blow. With a gasp she drops the tray. A cry
    of torment comes from her lips. She stands stunned)
  What is it? What's happened to her?
Fanny: Please. Please, don't look at her.
Mary: Charles? Charles? Where are you?
Charles: (leaving Fanny's side) I'm here, Mary.

Coleridge: (To those in the room caught between embarrass-
ment and morbid interest) If you don't mind . . . I think it
would be best if we leave Miss Lamb . . .
Mary: I thought it would never happen again. I thought I was
well. Oh, I am badly afraid that it is come.
Charles: I am here. Beside you, Mary.
Mary: See that Becky does not go to the bake shop in the morn-
ing. The loaves are fresher from the oven in the evening.
Charles: I will. I will. I will see to it.
Mary: And have *Emma* put away the Hogarth glasses. She
knows about them.
Charles: Yes. Yes, Mary.
Mary: And when the chimney sweepers come, have Becky tell
them—because I won't be there to tell them. Because I'll be
in Bedlam—in Bedlam. In Bedlam . . .
Charles: You will never be in Bedlam.
Coleridge: (The other guests are off now; only Fanny remains.
He stands on the threshold) Charles. Charles, can I help?
Charles: Please, please go.
    (Coleridge goes off)
Fanny: Charles, can't I help? Charles, won't you let me?
Mary: (Having been in the protective arms for a moment, she
breaks free. She moves away, peering; she speaks sleepily)
Oh, sir, your glass is empty.
    (Pointing to another empty chair)
Surely you'll have another cup of tea? And won't you all . . .
won't you all come have a little more roast pig? Charles is so
fond of roast pig. We had such good roast pig at Cambridge. I
expect they have the best roast pig in England there. That
young undergraduate we met there so enjoyed it—
Charles: Mary, for the love of God—
Mary: It was so pretty back at my grandmother's . . . All the
flowers . . . Charles put flowers in my hand tonight, but he
didn't give them to me. He used to give me flowers.
    (Now, Mary "halloo's" as if she were out of doors)
Charles. Charles! No, not those.
    (She motions him away)
The *double* daffodils—the curly ones with the green deep
down in the petals. Yes, that's right.

(She pauses a moment)

Ah, look, they're almost as tall as he is.

(Another pause; Charles has been running the flowers
back to her. She accepts an imaginary bouquet from him)

Ah, thank you, Charles.

(Pause)

No, Charles, no, dear little brother, this is the way it goes:
"Amo, Amas, Amat, Amamus, Amatis, Amant." I taught
you that, didn't I? It wasn't she who taught you.

(Pause)

I must go back to London, Charles . . . Back to Mother . . . I
don't want to . . . I don't want to . . . I can't stand being
hated; I can't stand it!

(She lifts her palms toward her face and shrieks)

Blood! Wet and sticky and red.

(She lowers them, wiping them on her gown)

Her blood! Oh, God! Her blood.

(Pause and a calm tone)

Yet, all through these years, when I see her face when I
dream, she looks kindly at me.

Fanny: Charles! Charles! Please—

Charles: (No attention to Fanny) I know, Mary, I know. Everyone loves you, Mary.

Mary: It doesn't matter if everyone loves you, if you are alone.
You and I were together . . . I think that's the most beautiful
word: together. Charles, we were together . . . in our work
. . . in our life . . . and with our friends. I love it that way,
Charles.

(She shakes under the weight of another fit)

I feel it coming . . . It's coming . . . It's coming . . . Tell
Becky about the bakers . . . Tell Emma about the glasses . . .
Oh, my God, Fanny! Oh, Charles, Charles, Charles . . . Don't
leave me. Please . . . please . . . please, don't leave.

Charles: Mary, no. I won't leave you. I know I can't. I'll always
stay with you. Oh, Christ, Christ, Christ, what else is there
for me to do?

(Fanny slowly turns and leaves the room)

Mary: Charles . . . Charles . . . It's coming . . . Quicker and
quicker, it's coming.

(Shrieks)
Don't leave me alone.

Charles: No, Mary, never as long as I live.

(Charles takes off his coat and brings it toward her. Mary puts her hands up, as if she were being helped on with a cape)

Mary: (Calmly) Charles, I must die first, you know.

Charles (He takes the coat and reverses it so that Mary puts her arms through the sleeves, back to front, so that it is in effect a restraining garment) Yes Mary, you must die first.

(Charles leads her off as if she were blind)

Curtain

ORIGINAL CAST AND STAFF OF

THE COAST OF ILLYRIA

The Coast of Illyria, by Dorothy Parker and Ross Evans, was given its world premier April 4–23, 1949, at the Theatre '49, Gulf Oil Theatre, Fair Grounds, Dallas, Texas. It was directed by Margo Jones, with Jonathan Seymour, Assistant Director; Jed Mace, Production Designer; and Richard Bernstein, Lighting.

Cast (in the order of their appearance)

Mary Lamb	Romola Robb
Charles Lamb	Wilson Brooks
Becky	Margaret McDonald
Emma Isola	Rebecca Hargis
Coleridge	Edwin Whitner
Fanny Kelly	Frances Waller
George Dyer	Harold Webster
Mrs. Kelly	Mary Finney
William Hazlitt	Clinton Anderson
Thomas De Quincey	John Hudson
Mrs. Crittenden	Edythe Chan
Mr. Crittenden	Jack Warden

Staff for Theatre '49:

Manning Gurian	Business Manager
J. B. Tad Adoue III	Company Manager
Mabel Duke	Watson Associates, Public Relations
Jed Mace	Costumes and Setting
Richard Bernstein	Technical Director
Marilyn Putnam	Technical Assistant
Jonathan Seymour	Stage Manager
Rebecca Hargis	Production Assistant
Charles Braswell	Production Assistant
Billie Baker	Treasurer

PROGRAM NOTES FOR THE

ORIGINAL PRODUCTION

ROMOLA ROBB (Mary Lamb) was born in Boston, educated at Radcliffe, studied and traveled in Europe . . . Began acting with Harvard Dramatic Club and Boston Repertory Company, played East Coast stock . . . Then to New York to play Nurse Ruth Kelly in "Harvey" with Frank Fay . . . In radio her voice is a familiar one on such programs as "Big Town," "Our Gal Sunday" and "Board of Missing Heirs."

WILSON BROOKS (Charles Lamb) returns to Theatre '49 after a season in "Command Decision" with Paul Kelly in New York and Chicago . . . He began acting in Cleveland stock, served with the Army Signal Corps during the war, and resumed his career in the New York revival of "Murder Without Crime," with John Carradine . . . Acted with the Dallas repertory theatre in its first two seasons.

FRANCES WALLER (Fanny Kelly) began her theatre career with New York Neighborhood Playhouse after receiving M.A. degree at Judson College, Alabama . . . On Broadway she played the ingenue leads in "Deep Are The Roots," replacing Barbara Bel Geddes, "Wonderful Journey" and "The Great Campaign" . . . Joined the Dallas company in November, 1947 . . . Last summer she was one of five professional actors, including Aline McMahon, chosen to head the Stanford University Drama Theatre summer season.

HAROLD WEBSTER (George Dyer) veteran actor of the New York stage, began career as piano accompanist for Emma Eames and David Bispham in concert, changed to acting and has played with leading stars of three decades, including Jane Cowl in "Smiling Through;" Philip Merivale in "Scotch Mist;" Ethel Barrymore in "The Second Mrs. Tanqueray;" Gertrude Lawrence in "Skylark;" Basil Rathbone and Violet Kemble Cooper in "Command To Love" and many others . . . Played in films with Gary Cooper in "Peter Ibbetson" and Mary Boland in "College Holiday."

REBECCA HARGIS (Emma Isola) has been on the staff of the Dallas repertory theatre since its opening, working chiefly in production and playing occasional roles . . . Received A.B. degree at University of Texas, followed by graduate study at Yale University . . . Acted and directed plays in Yale Drama Theatre, acted at Pasadena Playhouse and appeared in New York television . . . Last summer she was production adviser and lighting designer for the Reeder Children's Theatre, Fort Worth.

EDWIN WHITNER (Coleridge) studied at the American Academy of Dramatic Art . . . Played summer stock with Humphrey Bogart, Nydia Westman and Mary Phillips . . . On Broadway in "Houseparty," Arthur Hopkins' "The Magnificent Yankee" with Louis Calhern and Dorothy Gish, others . . . Played repertory with George Vivian and Jose Ferrer . . . Has done much radio work as actor and announcer . . . Previously visited Texas for basic training at Abilene, preceding three years with 67th General Hospital overseas.

MARY FINNEY (Mrs. Kelly) was the child of actors and has been in the theatre since infancy . . . Educated in Convent . . . Returned to the stage in her parents' stock company . . . Played with Frank Craven in New York, then to San Francisco radio, Pasadena Playhouse and West Coast theatres . . . Joined the Dallas company in November, 1947 . . . Last summer was principal actress of Holiday Theatre in Tustin, California.

CLINTON ANDERSON (William Hazlitt) studied for the stage at the University of Texas Drama School, toured the Southwest with Interstate Players . . . Played East Coast stock with Cornelia Otis Skinner, Charles Coburn, Frank Craven and June Walker . . . Acted in Chicago radio . . . was commentator for army training films at Hal Roach Studios while serving in Army Air Forces . . . Has been with the Dallas theatre since its first season.

JOHN HUDSON (Thomas De Quincey) was educated at San Mateo College, began acting with Henry Duffy's stock company in his native San Francisco . . . Played in Max Reinhardt's "Faust," played East Coast stock and then to Broadway in "Junior Miss," "The Eve of St. Mark," "January Thaw," "Craig's

Wife" and "The Men We Marry" . . . Interrupted his career during this period for three years service as an army pilot . . . Has acted in radio on the CBS and NBC networks.

JACK WARDEN (Mr. Crittenden) began acting after medical discharge from paratroops following injury in an overseas jump . . . Acted with Harold Winsten's touring repertory company, and studied with Miriam Goldina, former Stanislavsky pupil . . . He joined the Dallas theatre in its first season as a production assistant and last year became a member of the regular acting company . . . Last summer, played stock in Marblehead, Mass., and Long Island theatres.

SUPPLEMENTING the Theatre '49 acting company are two Dallas actresses, MARGARET MCDONALD (Becky) and EDYTHE CHAN (Mrs. Crittenden). Both are well known to local audiences through their appearances with the Dallas Little Theatre and the SMU Arden Club.

MARGO JONES (Managing Director) is an eminent producer-director in the New York theatre, but chooses to devote the majority of her time to the repertory theatre in Dallas . . . She is a native Texan, educated at Texas State College for Women, Denton . . . Directed Houston Community Players and Pasadena Playhouse Summer Theatre, taught one year in the University of Texas Drama School . . . Made world tour to study great repertory theatres of Europe, the British Isles and the Orient . . . Was granted a Rockefeller Fellowship to study repertory prospects in America . . . She chose Dallas as the ideal location for a permanent, professional repertory company . . . Dallas citizens contributed financially to establish the theatre here, and the first season was opened in June, 1947 . . . On the New York stage Miss Jones was co-director with Eddie Dowling of "The Glass Menagerie;" she directed "On Whitman Avenue" and Maxwell Anderson's "Joan of Lorraine" starring Ingrid Bergman, and Tennessee Williams' newest play, "Summer and Smoke."

April 4: 177 seats sold, 14 passes (seating capacity, 199), net proceeds of $368.16; April 5, 181 seats sold, net $376.48; April 6 (matinee), 129 seats sold, net $193.50; April 6 (evening), 196 seats sold, net $407.68; April 7, 196 seats sold, net $407.68; April 8, 190 seats sold, net $395.20; April 9 (matinee), 193 seats sold, $289.50; April 9 (evening), 198 seats sold, net $411.84; April 11, 185 seats sold, net $384.80; April 12, 196 seats sold, net $407.68; April 13 (matinee), 198 seats sold, net $297; April 13 (evening), 193 seats sold, net $401.44; April 14, 190 seats sold, net $395.20; April 15, 189 seats sold, net $393.12; April 16 (matinee), 198 seats sold, net $297; April 16 (evening), 198 seats sold, net $411.84; April 18, 185 seats sold, net $384.80; April 19, 160 seats sold, net $332.80; April 20 (matinee), 155 seats sold, net $232.50; April 20 (evening), 198 seats sold, net $411.84; April 21, 198 seats sold, net $411.84; April 22, 198 seats sold, net $411.84; April 23 (matinee), 198 seats sold, net $297; April 23 (evening), 198 seats sold, net $411.84; May 16, 118 seats sold, net $245.44; May 17, 112 seats sold, net $232.96; May 18 (matinee), 127 seats sold, net $190.50; May 18 (evening), 115 seats sold, net $239.20; May 28 (matinee), 196 seats sold, net $294; May 28 (evening), 180 seats sold, net $374.40; June 4 (matinee), 191 seats sold, net $286.50; June 4 (evening), 194 seats sold, net $403.52.

Totals: 32 performances; net proceeds regular season (April 4–23), $2850.04 (week 1); $2988.08 (week 2); $2894.46 (week 3); repertory season, $908.10 (week 1); $668.40 (May 28); $690.02 (June 4).

Weekly payroll (with actors at $75 gross): $1398.

ACT I. SCENE 5.

Mildred (Holding up bottle): I thought there was a drink left
in here, but no.

(Drops bottle into basket)

Irma: Ah, that doesn't do any good.

Mildred: Yes, it does, Irma. It makes you a different person.
You're not yourself for a little while and that's velvet. Let's
see.

(Goes over to the closet, takes out a second bottle with a
little whiskey remaining in it)

I was saving this for when I got really good and sunk. I guess
this is the time.

(Pours a drink)

Irma: I tell you it doesn't help.

Mildred: I tell you it does. A couple of drinks and I've got some
nerve. Otherwise I'm frightened all the time.

Irma (As to a child): Now what is there for you to be scared of?

Mildred: Everything. The dark; morning; tonight, tomorrow;
next week; forever.

Irma: You've got to look on the bright side. Things are going to
be all right.

Mildred: You've said that too often for me to believe it
anymore.

(Lights a cigarette, becomes aware of her hand shaking)

Look at that. That isn't whiskey. It's been shaking like that
for years—ever since the first time I saw what he really was
like.

Irma: There wasn't any mail outside. Did you take it in?

Mildred: There wasn't any to take in. It's the same old trick,
not sending the check.

Irma: Maybe it's gone astray, Mrs. Tynan?

Mildred: No, Irma, mail doesn't go astray. You know, heat and
snow and gloom of night and all that. No.

(A sudden outburst)
Oh, why doesn't the damn check come?

ACT I. SCENE 6.

Connie (Connie is at the mantelpiece and is studying Christopher's finger-painting): What in God's name is this?

Lulu: One of Christopher's finger-paintings.

Connie: Well, they say it would be a dreary world if everybody in it was talented.

Lulu: Connie, is there something wrong with me?

Connie: What, for instance?

Lulu: Well, I'm not really drawn to Christopher. I always thought children were charming, but this one seems to me a crashing little bore.

Connie: Why don't you tell Betsy she ought to have him destroyed?

Lulu: Shucks, I didn't think of it. And I could have used it last night. We had a rousing brawl. I'm not too proud of it.

Connie: What did Bob do?

Lulu: Looked miserable.

Connie: That must have been a help.

Lulu: You know, it was, somehow. Bob's so sweet. He's terribly worried about me. He thinks I'll go to pieces unless I find something to do.

Connie: He does, Lulu?

Lulu: Well, you know. Married sons will feel guilty about their mothers, Lord knows why. If only mother were standing up at a machine all day she wouldn't demand attentions. He simply can't realize that this mother doesn't.

Connie: I don't know. Sometimes people worry because they're really concerned . . . What else have you been doing? Have you met any of our ladies in the hotel?

ACT II. SCENE I.

The Corridor. It is several months later, a morning in March. Newspapers and mail are in front of each door. As the light comes up, Mrs. Lauterbach opens her door. She is again in a wrapper with her hair in curlers under a net. She picks up a

letter, quickly opens it. As she reads it, her face is trans-
formed; it is all smiles, and she even gives a little cry of delight. Quickly she goes to Mrs. Gordon's door, knocks on it.
As she stands waiting, Charles Nichols comes out of his door
to pick up the paper and mail.

Mrs. Lauterbach: Oh, good morning, Mr. Nichols. Your mother
have a good night?

Charles: I think so. She isn't awake yet.

Mrs. Lauterbach: Well, when she wakes up you tell her she's
just got to come down to the lobby this afternoon. I've got
some wonderful news.

Charles: I'll tell her, Mrs. Lauterbach.

(He goes into his room as Mrs. Gordon appears in her
wrapper)

Mrs. Gordon: Well, what's all this knocking and banging? I was
afraid you might be a telegram.

Mrs. Lauterbach: Oh, I didn't wake you up, did I?

Mrs. Gordon (Darkly): Well, I was up pretty late.

Mrs. Lauterbach: I just got such gorgeous news I had to tell you
right away.

(Indicates the letter)

From my daughter. She's pretty sure I can come up for
Easter. She doesn't think they're going any place.

Mrs. Gordon: Well, now that's real nice.

Mrs. Lauterbach: My, I'm going to have a lot to do. I want to
get presents for the children, and something for her, and for
my son-in-law. And then I'd really like to get some little
things for the maid—show I haven't forgotten her.

Mrs. Gordon: You're pretty sure you're going, aren't you?

Mrs. Lauterbach: Why, I don't think my daughter would say
this much unless she meant it. She knows how disappointed
I was at Christmas time.

Mrs. Gordon: Well, what's new on the Rialto?

Mrs. Lauterbach: Only this.

(Indicates the letter again)

Mrs. Gordon: Well, I got some news for you. At twenty minutes
past two o'clock this morning that young man was still in
Her Royal Highness's room.

Mrs. Lauterbach: Now how do you know that.

Mrs. Gordon: I'll tell you how I know that: I heard him in there.

Mrs. Lauterbach (Puzzled): You heard him from your room?

Mrs. Gordon: Well, Mrs. Lauterbach, I naturally want to know what kind of people we got living here on the corridor. So I just went out of my room and I walked past her door. I thought if anybody sees me, I'll just say I'm going to mail a letter. And I heard talking. I heard his voice just as plain.

Mrs. Lauterbach: If they were talking, it couldn't be anything bad.

Mrs. Gordon: Oh, no? They can talk afterwards, can't they? So I went back to my room and I don't know what time they *did* go.

Mrs. Lauterbach: Oh, dear. Well, maybe he was just sitting up with her, comforting her. She must feel terrible since that sweet little dog of hers died.

Mrs. Gordon: Some people only know one way of being comforted.

Mrs. Lauterbach: Oh, dear. And she with her son and his family. I don't see why anybody would want anything else.

Mrs. Gordon: Well, I could have told you. When she first came here I said to her—out of the goodness of my heart I said: "Honey, you get that other twin bed right out of your room. Nothing so lonesome as an empty bed beside you all night." So she let that bed stay right where it was. I reckon she knew she wasn't going to be lonesome.

(Irma comes by; she has her pail and brooms with her)

Irma: Good morning, Mrs. Lauterbach. Good morning, Mrs. Gordon.

Mrs. Gordon and *Mrs. Lauterbach* (Together): Good morning, Irma.

Mrs. Gordon: I see Mrs. Tynan has got that "do not disturb" sign on her door again. How many days is it now?

Mrs. Lauterbach: Anything the trouble with her, Irma?

Irma: She's just kind of tired out. She's just taking a rest for herself.

(Irma goes)

Mrs. Gordon: What does she need a rest for? One day from the next, she don't do one single thing.

Mrs. Lauterbach: I think I can trust Irma to come in and water my ivy while I'm away.

Mrs. Gordon: All tired out. What does she do to get tired about?

Mrs. Lauterbach: I think Irma's all right, don't you? But it's funny there's never been a sign of my little blue ashtray.

Mrs. Gordon: I don't see why she bothers to hang out that little old sign. I don't see so many people wanting to disturb her.

Mrs. Lauterbach: I don't like those "do not disturb" signs. I remember when I first came here there was an actress named Viola Hasbruch—big Shakespeare actress—

Mrs. Gordon: Yes, I know, Mrs. Lauterbach.

Mrs. Lauterbach: She just stayed right in her room all alone. And toward the last she had the "do not disturb" sign on so much that one day they went into see what was the matter and there she was—

Mrs. Gordon: Yes, honey, she was sitting there dead.

Mrs. Lauterbach (Bewildered): How did you know that?

Mrs. Gordon: You told me.

Mrs. Lauterbach: I did?

Mrs. Gordon: Now I got to get going. I got to get a manicure; and I want to stop at the bank; and I'm going to see if they can't fix that hat so it sets easier. See you later.

(She goes into her room. Mrs. Lauterbach looks at her puzzled, then goes into her own room)

Darkness

ACT II. SCENE 2.

Lulu: Where are you going?

Paul: Just to get a cigarette.

(Crosses to a table where there's a cigarette box)

Look, Lulu, the Pasons want to know if you'd like to come to dinner next Thursday.

Lulu: Why, were you talking about me?

Paul: Yes, I believe I mentioned you every few minutes. What about next Thursday?

Lulu: I don't think so, Paul.

Paul: Why?

Lulu: I've arranged to have a bad headache.

Paul: Oh, come on, Lulu. They want to meet you. And you'll like them.

Lulu: I'm sure they're lovely, but—Well, it would be like facing a police line-up. I don't want to be inspected, discussed and compared.

Paul: That's pretty silly.

Lulu: Well, it's the way I feel.

(She rises from the sofa, pats the pillow)

Did you say I'd go to the Pasons?

Paul: No, of course not. I said I'd ask you.

Lulu: Will you go if I don't go?

Paul: Yes, I think I will. But it's both of us they want.

Lulu: Do you plan to see them regularly from now on?

Paul: I hope so. It's sick to keep away from people. You taught me that. You're doing too much of it yourself, Lulu.

Lulu: But I don't want to see anybody but you.

Paul: Look, Lulu, two people, no matter what their feeling, mustn't feed entirely on each other . . . If they do, all that's left of them is a little heap of bones.

ACT II. SCENE 4.

The Lobby again. It is an April afternoon, a month later. When the light comes up we discover Mrs. Lauterbach at the desk speaking to Mr. Humphries. Mrs. Gordon is seated on the sofa carrying a lending library book. Harry is at his customary position near the desk. The ladies are still in dark blue, but in deference to the Spring each wears a little flowered hat and has replaced the mink cape with a small fur piece.

Mrs. Lauterbach (Gay and elated): Just regular stamps for these. But we've got to have an airmail for this one. I want it to get up to my daughter just as quick as it can possibly fly. Oh, and Mr. Humphries, the first thing tomorrow morning would you have my two suitcases taken out of the storeroom and brought up to me? I don't think I want the trunk. I think

the two suitcases will be enough for a ten-day visit, don't
you?

Mr. Humphries: I'm glad you're not going to be away from us
any longer.

Mrs. Lauterbach: Well, ten days will just about give me time to
get friends with my grandchildren. Just think, I haven't seen
them in a whole year and you know how kiddies change.

Mr. Humphries: I'm sure you'll have a lovely visit.

Mrs. Lauterbach: So am I. I just can't wait.

(She's stamped the envelopes and paid Mr. Humphries.
Now she turns to take the envelopes to the mailbox. Harry
steps forward)

Harry: I'll put those in the box for you, Mrs. Lauterbach.

Mrs. Lauterbach: Oh, thank you, Harry. Careful of this one.
This is the one that tells my daughter what time I'm
arriving.

(She watches Harry put the letters in the mailbox, then
goes to where Mrs. Gordon is seated)

Greetings, fair lady. I see you're holding the fort alone this
afternoon.

Mrs. Gordon: I thought you had just about deserted me.

Mrs. Lauterbach: I don't know what kind of company I'll be.
I'm so excited I don't know what I'm doing.

Mrs. Gordon: Mean thing, leaving me all alone for Easter.

Mrs. Lauterbach: That's the one thing I'm sorry about, missing
the Easter parade.

Mrs. Gordon: I believe I'll try to coax Mrs. Nichols to go to
church with me. Plenty of people go to church in wheel-
chairs. And if you're with a person who's lost the use of their
limbs they're apt to give you seats right on the aisle. I want
to get a good view of the hats. They say everything's going to
be flowers this year. You and I would be right in it.

Mrs. Lauterbach: Well, no need asking you what you've been
doing with yourself. I see where you've been.

(Touches the lending library book)

Did they say that was good at the library?

Mrs. Gordon: They say everything's good.

Mrs. Lauterbach: Yes, that's true. You have to read it yourself to
find out.

Mrs. Gordon: I gave the girl fair warning. If this is as bad as the last one I got I'm going to change libraries.

Mrs. Lauterbach: What else did you do?

Mrs. Gordon (Indicating book): This is all. I felt kind of tuckered out.

Mrs. Lauterbach: Well, I don't blame you, after that nasty experience yesterday. Do you think I ought to take my fur coat to Oswego? My daughter says it's often ten degrees colder up there than it is in New York. They don't have the Gulf Stream up there, you know.

Mrs. Gordon: A person don't recover from a thing like that so easy. It will be many a day before I throw it off.

Mrs. Lauterbach: But I don't know. I might lug it all the way up there, and never have any use for it.

Mrs. Gordon: I tossed and turned all night. It all came back to me just as vivid as I see you.

Mrs. Lauterbach: Still, if it turned cold. There I'd be. Maybe I'd better take it along over my arm. Look, here comes Her Royal Highness.

Mrs. Gordon: Getting out of a taxicab, just like anybody else.

Mrs. Lauterbach: I haven't seen that young man of hers so much lately. He must be away.

Mrs. Gordon: Away from her, anyway.

(Lulu enters from the direction of the street. She passes the ladies)

Lulu (Pleasantly): Good afternoon.

Mrs. Lauterbach (As Mrs. Gordon bows in silence): Good afternoon.

(Lulu goes to the desk while the ladies watch her intently)

Lulu: Good afternoon, Mr. Humphries. Are there any messages for me?

Mr. Humphries (Looking in her mailbox): I don't believe so, Mrs. Ames. No; nothing.

Lulu: Oh, dear. Are you sure?

Mr. Humphries (Indicating the pigeonholes): Nothing at all.

Lulu: Thank you.

(She starts away)

Mr. Humphries (To Casey, who is offstage): What, Casey? . . . Oh, Mrs. Ames!

Lulu (Coming back): Yes?

Mr. Humphries: There's a call for you now.

Lulu: Well, I'll go up to my room. Well, now. Let me take it
here, please.

(She picks up the house telephone. The ladies listen)
Hello . . . Ah, hello, Paul.

(Her voice drops into tenderness)
Oh, it's been such a long time . . . Sure it's a long time.
Twelve hours since last night. What are you doing? Busy? . . .
Oh, good, it's good for you. You know what I've been doing?
Three thousand guesses. Out buying all the records you like.
You'll have a field day. What time will you get here? . . . Oh,
Paul, no. Ah, no. Not for dinner really?

(Her voice is low; obviously she's disappointed)
Oh, well, just so long as it's going to be dull it's all right. But
you'll come up after, won't you . . . Oh, fine. We'll play all
the music and so forth. Thanks for calling, dear. Good-bye
for a little while.

(She hangs up, goes toward the elevator)

Mrs. Gordon: Well, did you hear that? Sounds like he's keeping
her waiting. Things are going to get kind of interesting
around here. Reckon you're sorry you're going away.

Mrs. Lauterbach: I hope everything goes all right for her. Glad
to see somebody get something. You know, Virginia, maybe
we've been kind of stand-offish too. Maybe we ought to ask
her to go to the movies again.

Mrs. Gordon: Oh, no, next time she's got to ask us. She'll come
crawling on her knees to us before I ask her again.

(Her attention has been drawn toward the elevator)
Well, well, well—

(Mrs. Nichols enters, being pushed by Charles. Charles is
right back where we saw him first: a small, weary man,
propelling his mother's chair)

Mrs. Lauterbach: Well, here she is—here her was. Greetings,
fair lady.

Mrs. Nichols: Well, this is very pleasant. Charles, don't you
want to push me just a little closer. Thank you, dear.

Mrs. Gordon: Well, you off again, Charles?

Mrs. Lauterbach: You hieing yourself off to the zoo?

(Charles, busy tucking the cover around his mother's knees, does not answer)

Mrs. Nichols: What's the matter, Charles? Cat got your tongue? Can't you answer the ladies?

Charles: Yes, I'm hieing myself off to the zoo again. Good afternoon.

(He goes)

Mrs. Gordon (Calling after him): Give my love to Rosie.

Mrs. Nichols: A little chilly down here, isn't it? They may have taken the revolving door off too soon.

Mrs. Lauterbach: I'm always glad to see it go. It means good-bye Old Mr. Winter.

Mrs. Nichols: Missed you yesterday, Mrs. Gordon. What happened to you?

Mrs. Gordon: What didn't happen!

Mrs. Nichols: Were you out buying that pretty hat? My, you ladies look so spring-like.

Mrs. Lauterbach: Oh, she had a terrible experience.

Mrs. Gordon: Little old dinky imitation pearl bracelet. Wasn't worth more than two dollars. Just tried it on there in the store—more for fun than anything—see how it would look on my arm. Then I started looking at other things and forgot all about it. When I'm going to the door, lo and behold, this detective comes strutting up to me and makes out like I'm trying to steal it.

Mrs. Nichols: No!

Mrs. Gordon: Well, sir, I gave him a piece of my mind. Yes, I told that little old sales girl something, too. "Look, here, Miss Too-Big-For-Your-Britches," I said to her, "customer's got a right to be forgetful, but you got a right to remind them. If I wasn't just a soft-hearted ninny," I said, "I could have you fired this minute."

Mrs. Nichols: What did she say to that?

Mrs. Gordon: What could she say? Well, they can keep their little old trumpery bracelet. I wouldn't give it house room.

Mrs. Nichols (Sympathetically): Well, try to forget the whole thing.

Mrs. Lauterbach: That's what I told her.

Mrs. Gordon: Well, I got to forget about it or I won't sleep

again tonight. Believe I'll start making up for last night right
now.

(Rises)

I'll give myself an extra half hour on my beauty rest. No
cheating today. All my clothes are going to come right off.
Mrs. Lauterbach, you come knock at my door when it's time
for us to start for Schrafft's. Mrs. Nichols, any chance of persuading you to come with us to the movies tonight?

Mrs. Nichols: Well, I'll talk it over with Charles. He's the boss
in this family, you know.

Mrs. Gordon: Well, you tell him it will break our hearts if he
don't come. I'll see you later, then.

(She goes toward the elevators)

Mrs. Lauterbach (After she's gone): Isn't that terrible what
happened to her about that bracelet?

Mrs. Nichols: If you believe it.

Mrs. Lauterbach: Of course, I warned her one day that she
would get caught.

Mrs. Nichols: Did you ever find that little blue ashtray?

Mrs. Lauterbach: It's just vanished into thin air.

(Then, with sudden understanding)

Oh, I don't think so, Mrs. Nichols. A big store is one thing,
but I don't think she'd do it to a friend.

Mrs. Nichols: Well—

(Before Mrs. Nichols can elaborate, Mildred enters from
the direction of the street. She carries the familiar paper
bag with the bottle in it. Mr. Humphries has returned to
the desk, and is busy writing. Mildred is so concentrating
on avoiding Mr. Humphries, that she does not see the
ladies and passes them without a word. The ladies look at
each other and shrug. Mildred is nearly past the desk, and
Mr. Humphries has not noticed her when Harry speaks
loudly)

Harry (A deep bow): Good afternoon, Mrs. Tynan.

Mr. Humphries (Looking up): Oh, Mrs. Tynan, just a minute.

(He comes around from behind the desk. Reluctantly
Mildred comes back to meet him. They are standing
within earshot of Harry, who does not move)

Mildred: I know what you're going to say, Mr. Humphries.

Mr. Humphries: I'm afraid you do, Mrs. Tynan. I'm afraid it's a
rather old story by now.

Mildred: It certainly is, and I'm just as tired of it as you are.

Mr. Humphries: If there was just something you could do—

Mildred: Mr. Humphries, if there was something I could do I
would have done it long ago. I'm sure you know that.

Mr. Humphries: I do, Mrs. Tynan. It's only that it looks so bad
on the books, time after time like this.

Mildred: I should think you would get used to it, Mr. Humphries. But you don't. Neither do I!
    (Then, with sudden resolution)
Look, Mr. Humphries, look! As soon as my check comes I'll
pay up completely—everything.

Mr. Humphries: You've said that before, Mrs. Tynan.

Mildred: But this time I will. I really will. Well, there isn't
anything you want to say to me, is there?

Mr. Humphries: I'm afraid there is. There have been several
complaints recently.

Mildred: About what?

Mr. Humphries: Well—about this—
    (Indicates the bag in Mildred's hand)

Mildred: Oh . . . Good heavens, Mr. Humphries, I never go out
of my own room.

Mr. Humphries: The singing . . . sometimes it is a little . . . if
you could keep it softer.

Mildred: I will.
    (Turns to Mrs. Nichols and Mrs. Lauterbach)
Thank you for your kind attention, ladies. Always glad to
break the monotony.
    (She smiles at the ladies and goes. Before Mrs. Nichols and
Mrs. Lauterbach can recover—)
                    Darkness

ACT II. SCENE 5.

Connie: I'm sailing Friday on one of the Queens. I'm so excited
I don't remember which one. It could be Victoria for all I
know. And do you know what else? When I come back I'm
going to be a partner.

Lulu: That's wonderful.

Connie: Sure, it is, but I'll have to realize that later. I'm too excited about going to think about coming back. I honestly don't know what I'm doing. For God's sake, give me a drink to sober me up.

Lulu: I'll bring it to you. Sit down, dear.

Connie: Couldn't; couldn't.

(Begins to wander about the room)

This really is a successful room. The table looks lovely.

(Picks up a spoon)

Lulu Ames, did you buy new silver? It's beautiful. It must have cost like all hell.

Lulu: I just got enough for two.

Connie: Oh . . . How is the gentleman?

Lulu (Handing Connie a drink): Fine, I guess. So busy I haven't seen much of him.

(She goes to window, looks down)

Connie, do you really think it matters that a woman is older than a man?

Connie (A little too heartily): Not one bit! What's youth anyway? An accident of birth. A matter of timing on the part of your parents.

Lulu (Moving away from the window): Paul doesn't think about it. I'm the one who does.

Connie: Then stop.

Lulu: I've never felt so young. I've never been so young. I know it's bound to come—it's bound to catch up with me sometime. Oh, but not yet. I could still have two good years with Paul. Two perfect years. Maybe three . . . You do like Paul, don't you, Connie?

Connie: Just for myself I think he's very attractive. For you, if you love him, I do too.

Lulu: Oh, I do, I do, I do.

(She's again at the window)

Nasty little thing. He's late again. I always stand here to see him when he comes around the corner. He knows I'm here.

Connie: Are you worried?

Lulu: Yes, I am. Every time he's late I think he's met somebody else he likes better and I go right out of my mind.

Connie (Smiling): And you're going to have two perfect years.
Lulu: Oh, I'm not really worried.
>(Moves away from the window)
>It's just that I hate waiting so. I seem to have been doing
>quite a little of it lately.
Connie: That's no good. You must go out, Lulu.

.   .   .   .

Lulu (Going to the telephone): I can't stand this. I'm going to
find out where he is.
Connie: No, dear, no.
>(Connie takes the telephone away from Lulu)
>How many times have you telephoned him today?
Lulu: Three, four, I don't know. What do you care? Please give
me the telephone.
Connie: Stop it, Lulu. Stop smothering him.
Lulu: Give it to me! Give it to me!
>(Then when she sees Connie will not give her the phone
>she turns away angrily)
>You're a hard woman. You're a bad friend . . . Oh, Connie,
>what shall I do? If I lose him I'll die.
>(She begins to cry)
Connie: You'll do no such thing. Stop that talk.
Lulu: It's been a whole week.
Connie: And stop taking it this way. Do you imagine you're the
only one in the world who has gone to bed with a man she's
not married to?
Lulu: You don't have to put it that way. Do you think that's all
this is?
Connie: I think that's certainly most of it.

.   .   .   .

Paul: Good evening, Mrs. Ames.
>(He kisses her on the cheek)
Lulu: Oh, don't let yourself go too far . . . I'm sorry.
>(Then with determined good humor)
>What's the matter? Do you hate to see a woman drink?
Paul: Oh, I didn't see you didn't have one.
>(Throughout the rest of the scene, Paul tries to remain
>polite)
Lulu: Aren't you going to notice our table?

Paul: I did. It looks charming.

Lulu: And you wanted to ruin the whole effect by setting another place.

   (Touches a flower)

I've developed quite a drag with the chef since you were here last. No menus tonight. It's going to be something rather special. Who did you go to the cocktail party with?

Paul: I went alone. I didn't stay long.

Lulu: Who was there?

Paul: Quantities of people.

Lulu: Old friends of yours and Sally's?

Paul: Some of them, yes. The Pasons were there. They asked for you.

Lulu: Did you tell them you were coming here?

Paul: Why, no.

Lulu: Oh, I see. It wasn't anything you were proud of.

Paul: I thought this was going to be a nice evening.

Lulu: It is! It will be, I promise you! Oh, Paul, I don't know what gets into me. Let's start over. You're looking unusually handsome.

Paul: You're looking usually lovely.

   (They sit down together on the sofa)

That's a wonderful piece of luck for Connie Mercer. But you'll miss her, won't you?

ACT II. SCENE 6.

Mildred (Gay and high and talking to her image in the mirror): What will we drink this one to? All right, to us again. Me here and you there.

   (Toasts herself)

I wished we looked prettier, but we don't. All right, we were pretty once. What does it matter? It matters a lot I guess. It matters you get old. I didn't mean to get old this way. I never had to look at you except to be told how pretty I was. And now here I am. I'm a mess, mess, mess, mess, mess, mess. Ya-ah! All right, so we don't look so good, but we're better off than we were when I'd look at you and see his face over my shoulder.

   (Drinks)

That was just fine, that was great! Oh, wasn't he handsome;
wasn't he wonderful; oh, wasn't I a lucky girl that he married me! Yeah, sure! Sure it was fine! All that money. WHEEE!
All that money. I have to laugh now about the time I found
out what he was. Dirty man! Dirty man! Remember me, the
night I left him. Not a nickel. But I went to that hotel and
signed his name just to be there overnight. Then I didn't
know what to do. Remember? Now how would I know what
to do. Leaving that rich pig in that rich house. I came back
there in the morning; just wanted to get my clothes, and the
butler came to the door. I thought he was my friend, the
butler—and he said: "I'm sorry, Mrs. Tynan, but Mr. Tynan
has left orders you are not to be admitted." Oh, that was
funny! It was funny going to the pawnshop, wasn't it? I
didn't know where any pawnshops were. Asking a police-
man, that was funny. Yea, that diamond and sapphire bracelet. All right, so it got me the fare to New York, didn't it?
That was as far as I could get away from him in this country,
wasn't it? Ah, let's not talk about this anymore. Let's have
some fun, shall we?

   (Raises the glass again)

Come on.

   (She starts singing "Anchors Aweigh" off-key and
   raucously)

I wish I knew the words, but that doesn't matter.

.   .   .   .

ACT II. SCENE 7.

Mrs. Lauterbach: Good morning, fair lady. Sleepest thou well
   or sleepest thou ill?

Lulu (Smiling): I sleepest fair. That's the best I do.

Mrs. Gordon (Suspiciously): You take those sleeping pills?

Lulu: The doctor gave me some tablets, very mild.

Mrs. Gordon: I suppose he knows what he's doing. I wouldn't
   take one of those things if I had to stay on my feet all night.

Lulu: Ladies . . . I just wondered . . . if you haven't anything to
   do today . . . would you have lunch with me?

Mrs. Gordon: When we go out together, Mrs. Ames, we go
   Dutch.

Lulu: Yes, but just today, let me invite you. Won't you come?

Mrs. Gordon: Well—I'm sure that's real sweet.

Mrs. Lauterbach: I'd be glad to, Mrs. Ames.

Lulu: Oh, that's nice.

Mrs. Lauterbach: We haven't seen very much of you,
Mrs. Ames.

Lulu: I haven't been very well.

Mrs. Lauterbach: I guess your children keep you busy, too.

Lulu: They don't live in New York anymore—but my son
comes in to see me every Wednesday.

Mrs. Gordon: Yes, I've noticed that. Just as regular.

Lulu: He brought me new photographs of my grandchildren.
You must come in and see them. That baby girl is darling.

Mrs. Lauterbach: You going to spend Thanksgiving with them I
expect.

Lulu: I don't know yet.

Mrs. Gordon: Oh, dear. All the ladies going away for Thanksgiving with their families and I'll be left sitting alone in the
lobby with Harry and Mr. Humphries. Kind of hope you
don't go, Mrs. Ames. Hope you help me hold the fort.

Mrs. Lauterbach: Now, Virginia Gordon, you let her go. She'd
get a real joy out of being with those babies. You go, Mrs.
Ames, and you stay just as long as you can.

Lulu: We don't have to decide yet, do we? Then it's all right for
lunch, ladies?

Mrs. Gordon: Yes, but just this time, you know.

Lulu: I thought maybe after lunch . . . I have a card . . .
Sophie is showing her new collection of clothes . . . we
might go in and look at them for a while.

Mrs. Lauterbach: Oh, that would be nice.

Mrs. Gordon: My, that will be a full afternoon.

Mrs. Lauterbach: Maybe tonight you'd like to go with us to see
that new movie. It's got awfully good reviews.

Lulu: I'd love to, if you'd let me come with you.

Mrs. Gordon: Certainly will. What you doing this morning?

Lulu: I thought I'd go to the needlepoint shop. I need some
more of that deep rose wool.

Mrs. Gordon: Well, we'll go right along with you and help you
pick it out.

Lulu: Oh, thank you.

(The curtain begins to fall slowly)

The whole day is filled up, isn't it? I'm so glad. I do dread a day with nothing to do.

[FINAL] *Curtain*